ENVIRONMENTAL RESEARCH

AND DEVELOPMENT

STRENGTHENING THE
FEDERAL INFRASTRUCTURE

DECEMBER 1992

A Report of the

CARNEGIE COMMISSION
ON SCIENCE, TECHNOLOGY, AND GOVERNMENT

ISBN 1-881054-05-5

Printed in the United States of America

CONTENTS

FOREWORD   7

PREFACE   9

THE ENVIRONMENTAL CHALLENGE: SUMMARY AND   11
RECOMMENDATIONS
    S&T as Sources of Innovation, 12
    Improving the Federal Effort, 13
    Recommendations, 14
    The Way Forward, 22

PART I.   R&D FOR THE ENVIRONMENT

1. THE ENVIRONMENTAL CHALLENGES OF TODAY AND TOMORROW   27
    People and Global Environmental Change, 29
    Population Growth and Increasing Consumer Demand, 29

Scale of Environmental Damage, 30
Economic Benefits, Environmental Costs, 30
The Key Role of Environmental R&D, 31
S&T as Sources of Innovation, 31
Natural and Social Sciences, 32
Global Effort Needed, 33
Goals and Priorities, 34
An Effective Federal Environmental R&D Program, 34

2. THE PRESENT R&D SYSTEM: WHY IMPROVEMENTS   35
   ARE NECESSARY
   R&D Missions of the Major Departments and Agencies, 35
   Improving the Federal R&D Effort, 36
   Weaknesses of the Present System, 39
   Technology Development, 42
   U.S. Technology Policy and the Environment, 45
   Matching Resources with Problems, 45
   Organizational Considerations, 46

PART II.   RECOMMENDATIONS FOR STRENGTHENING THE
           FEDERAL ENVIRONMENTAL R&D SYSTEM

3. INTRODUCTION   55

4. LEADERSHIP AND THE RESEARCH AGENDA   57
   The Office of Environmental Quality, 58
   Institute for Environmental Assessment, 59
   Environmental Research and Monitoring Initiative, 60
   Office of Science and Technology Policy, 61

5. STRENGTHENING THE FEDERAL R&D INFRASTRUCTURE   62
   Environmental Protection Agency, 63
   Environmental Monitoring Agency, 72
   National Center for Environmental Information, 76
   Environmental Technologies Program, 78
   National Aeronautics and Space Administration, 79
   National Institute of Environmental Health Sciences, 81
   Department of the Interior, 82
   National Park Service, 82
   Bureau of Land Management, 83
   Department of Agriculture, 84
   Department of Energy National Laboratories, 86
   Department of Defense, 89
   Hazardous Waste R&D, 90

6. LINKING AND COORDINATING PROGRAMS 92
   Strengthening Linkages, 93
   International Cooperation, 94
   Multidisciplinary Communication and Collaboration, 97
   Links with Nongovernmental Organizations, 99
   Links with Industry, 101

7. BUILDING A STRONG INTELLECTUAL BASE 104
   National Science Foundation, 104
   Improving Education, 105

8. CONCLUSION: KNOWLEDGE AND LEADERSHIP FOR THE FUTURE 107
   Knowledge and Progress, 107
   Supporting Agency Missions, 108
   Assessment, Strategic Planning, and Policy Development, 108
   Better Monitoring and Information Storage, 109
   Maintaining a Strong Science and Technology Base, 110
   Creating Linkages, 110
   The Importance of Leadership, 111
   The Paradox of Progress, 111

APPENDIXES
   A. FEDERAL ENVIRONMENTAL R&D PROGRAMS 115
   B. BIOGRAPHIES OF TASK FORCE MEMBERS 130

NOTES AND REFERENCES 135

Members of the Carnegie Commission on Science, 141
   Technology, and Government

Members of the Advisory Council, Carnegie Commission on 142
   Science, Technology, and Government

Members of the Task Force on the Organization of Federal 143
   Environmental R&D Programs

FOREWORD

Environmental protection is an issue that cuts across the missions of more than a dozen major federal departments and agencies. Consequently, environmental research and development programs are highly decentralized, and directing and coordinating these diverse efforts is a particular challenge for policymakers.

Few would disagree that environmental protection and sustainable development will be among the highest priorities on the national agenda in the decades ahead. Since research and development programs will generate much of the intellectual basis for the environmental policies and actions of the future, it is essential that these programs be well organized, adequately funded, and closely linked with the policymaking process.

The earth may be viewed as an interacting set of complex biological and physical systems, and a host of human actions can adversely affect them. Consequently, federal environmental R&D encompasses a broad range of programs housed in numerous departments and agencies.

Today, the federal environmental R&D system is a loose collection of laboratories and programs, most of which were established to respond to the problems and priorities of the past. While many of these problems remain today, we also face a new set of challenges, and responding to them requires a more dynamic, interrelated organizational structure and more effective assessment and policymaking processes.

Over the past two years, a task force of the nation's leading experts on environmental R&D focused their attention on the organizational and decision-making needs of the federal government in this area. Their findings and recommendations, presented in this report, were adopted by the Carnegie Commission in September of 1992.

More than three decades ago, President John F. Kennedy spoke eloquently of the challenge facing the nation and the world: "It is our task in our time and in our generation to hand down undiminished to those who come after us, as was handed down to us by those who went before, the natural wealth and beauty which is ours."* This report was developed in that spirit.

William T. Golden, Co-Chair
Joshua Lederberg, Co-Chair

---

* Address at the dedication ceremonies of the National Wildlife Federation Building, March 3, 1961.

PREFACE

This report was approved by the Carnegie Commission on Science, Technology, and Government in September of 1992. It was prepared by the Task Force on the Organization of Federal Environmental R&D Programs:

Robert W. Fri, Co-Chair
H. Guyford Stever, Co-Chair
Douglas M. Costle
Edward A. Frieman
Stephen J. Gage
Bruce W. Karrh
Gordon J. F. MacDonald

Gilbert S. Omenn
David P. Rall
Gilbert F. White

Mark Schaefer, Senior Staff
Associate

The Task Force wishes to thank Steven J. Kafka, special consultant to the Task Force, for his extensive contributions to this report, particularly his thorough analysis of existing federal environmental R&D programs. We thank Michael Kowalok and Paul Locke for their excellent analytical assistance. We are grateful to Jeffrey Porro for providing the Task Force with research and editorial assistance, to commission staff member Jeannette Aspden for editing the final document, to A. Bryce Hoflund and Jane Godshalk for assistance in producing the final report, and to Bonnie Bisol for aiding in the report release and distribution. We would also like to express our appreciation to Kathy Gramp and her colleagues at the American Association for the Advancement of Science for their thorough analysis of federal funding for environmental R&D.

We wish to thank Jesse Ausubel, Jonathan Bender, David Beckler, and David Robinson for their helpful suggestions throughout the task force's work. We also thank Harvey Brooks, J. Clarence Davies, Jeanne Gorman, and K. Elaine Hoagland for providing the Task Force with helpful comments and suggestions.

THE ENVIRONMENTAL CHALLENGE:
SUMMARY AND RECOMMENDATIONS

Over the past three decades considerable progress has been made in recognizing the seriousness of the world's environmental problems. Although many positive steps have been taken to ameliorate them, we are only beginning to understand the complexities of the problems we face. In the years ahead, continuing struggle is likely because the two most significant forces of environmental degradation — the ever-growing world population and the drive for worldwide industrial and agricultural development — continue unabated.

The pressing and widespread threats to the biosphere appear more closely linked with the functioning of the world economy than they ever have before. Today's global economy has reinforced the geographic separation of resource extraction, production, and consumption. Hence, those who reap the economic benefits of using natural resources are often different from those who bear the environmental costs. This complex of issues was brought into sharper focus by the preparations for the United Nations Conference on Environment and Development in Rio de Janeiro in June 1992 and by the conference itself. This new awareness led to an international agenda for research on environment and development and various non-binding agreements, but much more must be done to stem global environmental degradation.

S&T AS SOURCES OF INNOVATION

Our ability to respond to the environmental and economic challenges of today and tomorrow is strongly dependent on the quality of the information produced by a well-organized and productive federal research and development system.

This report addresses the research and development organizations and the decision-making processes that the federal government needs to enable it to work toward national and global environmental objectives. Until recently, a "catch up, clean up" approach has dominated U.S. environmental policies. Little attention has been paid to developing a proactive analytical and policymaking system that can identify trends, anticipate problems, and address causes instead of symptoms. Our policies are beginning to change, but leadership and innovative approaches to solving problems based on strong research and development programs are essential.

More than twenty years ago the first images of the surface of the earth as seen from the moon helped people to visualize our planet as a unit, an integrated set of systems—landmasses, atmosphere, oceans, the plant and animal kingdoms—and to realize that threats to one could harm them all. Since then, considerable progress has been made in solving some of the problems facing the biosphere, but other threats to the environment persist, and new ones have emerged: the thinning of the ozone layer, the destruction of the rain forests, climate change, the contamination of groundwater, and new threats to wetlands, farmland, and other renewable resources. Most of our problems are due to human actions, especially those related to population growth and increased consumption of resources. These problems pose a special challenge to the world's scientific and engineering communities, one that evokes the image of the first human steps on the moon: Can scientists and engineers generate the kind of large-scale and highly focused effort that took us into space and apply it to developing the understanding necessary to protect our global environment?

The environmental challenges that we face today demand a concerted international effort. Our ability to respond to these challenges is defined by what research is conducted, how it is organized, and how well it is presented and used in establishing and implementing environmental policy. A wide range of research advances will be needed if "sustainable development" is to be achieved — growth that is a product of efficient consumption of energy and materials, minimizing waste and maximizing recycling, stabilizing land use, and assuring growth that does not damage the future environment on which further growth depends.

The United States must play a leading role in this effort, and doing so requires a vital, well-integrated federal environmental R&D system. Unfortunately, the existing federal environmental R&D infrastructure was built for another time and for a set of issues that no longer correspond to today's problems. If the federal government is to provide the scientific resources and leadership that a national and global environmental protection effort requires, a careful examination and rethinking of its R&D effort is essential.

IMPROVING THE FEDERAL EFFORT

At first glance, the federal environmental research enterprise seems impressive. More than a dozen federal departments and agencies conduct environment-related R&D; total spending is some $5 billion a year (see Tables 1 and 2 on pages 37 and 38). The bulk of these expenditures is devoted to the physical sciences, with most of the remainder directed to engineering and the biological and health sciences (see Figure 1 on page 37). Largely because of its origins as a series of individual programs initiated in response to specific problems, much of our current R&D system is diffuse, reactive, and focused on short-range, end-of-the-pipe solutions. And, because mechanisms to coordinate the products of environmental research conducted by federal, state, academic, and nongovernmental institutions are weak, it is difficult to develop the comprehensive information necessary to evaluate significant changes in the state of the environment.

Today's complicated and urgent environmental challenges cannot be addressed in the piecemeal fashion of the past. At a time of intense international economic competition and growing federal budget deficits, careful matching of resources with problems is vital. The end of the Cold War and limitations on defense spending offer opportunities to focus more attention on other societal needs, such as environmental protection. We believe that the federal environmental R&D effort must be broadened, its agencies and programs better coordinated, and its resources more focused on identifying root causes and anticipating emerging problems. As a nation, we face enormous environmental challenges. Strong and effective federal R&D programs are a prerequisite to attacking these problems successfully and, in doing

so, providing hope and a means of action for today's generation and those
of the future.

RECOMMENDATIONS

If the federal government is to meet the environmental and natural resources
challenges of the future, the distribution of R&D responsibilities across all
departments and agencies must be rethought. Key guiding organizational
considerations include effective support of department and agency missions;
a capacity to conduct strategic planning, anticipate future R&D needs, and
undertake comprehensive policy analyses; effective monitoring, information
storage, and retrieval capabilities; a strong science and technology base; and
effective linkages with other federal and international environmental R&D
programs. Our recommendations that follow are grouped into four broad
categories:

- Leadership and the research agenda
- Strengthening the federal R&D infrastructure
- Linking and coordinating programs
- Building a strong intellectual base

LEADERSHIP AND THE RESEARCH AGENDA

Leadership starts at the top, and the Executive Office of the President needs
new mechanisms to foster cooperation between departments and agencies
in their efforts to address high-priority problems. The President relies upon
several entities within the Executive Office in setting the research agenda.
These organizations must be strengthened in order to provide effective analysis
and advice to the President on environmental issues.

- **The White House apparatus for establishing environmental policy and
for guiding federal environmental R&D programs should be strengthened
by expanding the responsibilities of the existing units in the Executive Office
of the President and by establishing a new institutional capability to assess
scientific and technical information and analyze environmental issues from
the standpoint of economic, social, and political considerations.**

- *The mission of the existing White House Office of Environmental Quality
(OEQ) should be expanded, giving it broad responsibility for developing*

environmental policies in the context of other considerations, particularly economic. The office should also work to identify ways in which the activities of all federal departments and agencies can be directed toward sustainable development and risk-reduction objectives.

The Council on Environmental Quality (CEQ) was established by the National Environmental Policy Act in 1969. Shortly afterward, the White House Office of Environmental Quality (OEQ) was established by the Environmental Quality Improvement Act of 1970. CEQ has always been the dominant organizational entity. However, over the past four years, CEQ has operated not as a council, but as an office administered by a chairman who also serves as the director of OEQ. We believe that the activities of CEQ should be integrated into the Office of Environmental Quality. We considered other organizational mechanisms to provide a focal point for environmental policymaking in the White House. Building on the existing OEQ, rather than establishing an entirely new entity is, in our view, the most efficient approach.

We believe that OEQ's mission should be expanded and that it should be administered by a director who serves simultaneously as the Assistant to the President for the Environment. In this capacity the director should lead efforts in the White House to develop environmental policy options, presenting proposals to the President and the Cabinet for their consideration. The director should also be responsible for looking across all departments and agencies and identifying ways in which federal activities can be directed toward the environmental objectives of the President.

As discussed in an earlier Commission report, actions should be taken "to assure the stable and sustained functioning of a high-level mechanism concerned with linking environment, energy, and the economy."[1] OEQ should work with OSTP to identify major R&D needs, to promote the improvement of risk assessment and risk management procedures, and to coordinate major R&D initiatives. In addition, OEQ should work closely with the Office of Management and Budget in guiding the budget process with respect to environmental programs.

■ *An Institute for Environmental Assessment (IEA) should be established to evaluate global and national environmental problems and to develop alternative approaches to them.* The federal government currently lacks a critical mass of individuals who can assess the information resulting from our natural science research efforts in the context of current economic, social, and political considerations. We recommend the establishment of an Institute for Environmental Assessment dedicated to the evaluation of global and national environmental problems, the analysis of research and monitoring data pertaining to them, the assessment of emerging environmental technologies, and the development of economic, legal, and social analyses to aid in the development of environmental and risk-related policies. The institute should be administered by a director who reports to the Director of the White House Office of Environmental Quality (OEQ), or, alternatively, to the Secretary of a Department of the Environment.

We recommend that the IEA be provided with funds to undertake analysis within the institute itself and to support the work of individuals and institutions outside of the federal government through grants and contracts. At least half the institute's funding should be devoted to extramural studies conducted within nongovernmental organizations and academic institutions. Depending on its size and mission, an IEA could be located in the Executive Office, or in the Environmental Protection Agency or a proposed Department of the Environment. Alternatively, it could function as a quasigovernmental institution operated by a nongovernmental organization but reporting to the OEQ in the Executive Office.

■ *The President, with the guidance and support of Congress, should undertake an Environmental Research and Monitoring Initiative, a long-term effort to bring all federal environmental R&D programs into a common policy framework.* The Initiative should be guided by the Director of the Office of Environmental Quality and the Director of the Office of Science and Technology Policy and should involve the key administrators of federal R&D programs, as well as the Office of Management and Budget. The group should work to devise coherent short- and long-term R&D plans for each agency and department, including explicit goals and milestones.[2] Such an initiative could be a component of a broader National Environmental Strategy, which we understand the National Commission on the Environment will recommend in their upcoming report.[3]

■ *The Office of Science and Technology Policy should coordinate a broader array of environmental R&D activities.* The Office of Science and Technology Policy (OSTP) within the Executive Office of the President is the science advisory unit of the White House, and is home to the Federal Coordinating Council on Science, Engineering, and Technology (FCCSET). The Council has proved to be an effective mechanism for coordinating the management of certain federal R&D programs. We recommend that OSTP use FCCSET to aid in the development of coherent federal environmental R&D programs and to address problems that cut across departments and agencies. Close interaction between OSTP as it coordinates R&D programs, the Office of Environmental Quality as it develops environmental policy and identifies research needs, and the Office of Management and Budget as it devises budget priorities, is essential if the federal government is to achieve an integrated, forward-looking environmental protection program.

STRENGTHENING THE FEDERAL R&D INFRASTRUCTURE

Our federal environmental R&D system is broad, diverse, and highly decentralized. There is a need to strengthen the individual and collective R&D efforts at the nine major departments and agencies with environmental R&D programs, and to expand their capacity to contribute to the evaluation and implementation of environmental policies.

- **The federal environmental R&D infrastructure should be strengthened by improving and streamlining EPA's existing laboratory organization, by supporting a group of nonfederal Environmental Research Institutes, by organizing a new U.S. Environmental Monitoring Agency and a National Center for Environmental Information, and by enhancing R&D capabilities in several key federal agencies** (see pages 63–91).

- *The Environmental Protection Agency's existing laboratory structure, now comprised of 12 laboratories, should be consolidated to create a National Ecological Systems Laboratory, a National Environmental Monitoring Systems Laboratory, a National Environmental Engineering Laboratory, and a National Health Effects Research Laboratory.* We recommend several substantial changes in the EPA laboratory structure to accommodate the growing need for integrated environmental systems research and monitoring. The first is the incorporation of EPA's six environmental processes and effects laboratories into a single national laboratory with multiple field locations. The second is the merging of EPA's two environmental monitoring support laboratories and the agency's other monitoring activities into a single national laboratory.[4] (See Figure 6 on page 77). In addition, EPA's environmental engineering laboratories should be merged to form a single laboratory. The existing Health Effects Research Laboratory should be upgraded and designated a National Health Effects Research Laboratory.

- *EPA should establish and support up to six major Environmental Research Institutes (ERIs) associated with academic institutions and nongovernmental organizations across the country.* EPA's current Centers of Excellence program supports four university-based Environmental Research Centers (ERCs), each specializing in a particular research topic of agency interest. The work of the ERCs is severely limited by inadequate funding, currently averaging about $1 million per center per year.

   We believe that this program should be phased out and replaced with a set of major Environmental Research Institutes. In order to have a real impact on the environmental challenges facing the nation and the world, we believe that funding for each ERI should gradually rise to the level of $10 to $15 million annually for at least five years. We further propose that, after considering the views of a full range of experts from within and outside government, the EPA Science Advisory Board make recommendations to the EPA Administrator regarding the missions of the institutes.

The institutes should operate cooperatively with the four EPA National Laboratories described above. It might be advantageous to choose problem-oriented themes for the institutes that cut across the missions of the intramural National Laboratories. Since the institutes should operate on a five-year cycle, this would allow the periodic modification of the institutes' priorities. In this manner, the institutes would function as a more flexible, problem-oriented, multidisciplinary component of the EPA or a proposed Department of the Environment, thereby complementing the structured, discipline-oriented, intramural National Laboratories. We envision a two-way flow of personnel between the National Laboratories and the institutes. This would give government scientists and engineers — and social scientists — an opportunity to benefit from the career growth and educational opportunities offered in the university setting. It would also enhance the National Laboratories by bringing some of the best scientists and engineers in the nation into government laboratories for extended periods.

■ *A new federal agency, the U.S. Environmental Monitoring Agency (EMA), should be organized by combining the National Oceanic and Atmospheric Administration (NOAA), now within the Department of Commerce, with the U.S. Geological Survey (USGS), now within the Department of the Interior.* Monitoring, mapping, inventorying, and forecasting with respect to our national and the global environment are the cornerstones of our federal environmental protection efforts. The present and future missions of NOAA and USGS are more similar to each other than they are to the missions of the departments in which they now reside. We believe that both organizations would operate more effectively together.

The proposed Environmental Monitoring Agency should maintain close ties with the National Aeronautics and Space Administration in order to link NASA Earth Observing System (EOS) and related environmental monitoring efforts with its own activities. The EMA should make use of data from a wide range of other agencies, including EPA, the Fish and Wildlife Service, and the National Institute for Environmental Health Services. We believe that the EMA could operate as an independent federal agency; however, if a Department of the Environment is established, the EMA should be part of it.[5]

■ *A National Center for Environmental Information (NCEI) should be established within the proposed U.S. Environmental Monitoring Agency.* Such a center would serve as a focal point for the storage and retrieval of environmental information generated from a range of sources, primarily federal departments and agencies, but also state and local governments, academia, industry, and nongovernmental organizations. The Center should be responsible for developing policies to ensure that environmental data are properly stored and readily accessible to all users (see pages 76–78). The NCEI should build strong ties with the National Library of Medicine (NLM), whose Board of Regents recently approved expansion of its efforts in toxicology and environmental health.[6]

The R&D capabilities of several key federal agencies should be strengthened. The following recommendations are discussed in more detail in the report:

■ *A federal interagency Environmental Technologies Program should be established to promote and support the development of advanced technologies by federal agencies, universities, industry, and nongovernmental organizations* (see pages 78–79).

■ *The National Aeronautics and Space Administration should link its environmental monitoring activities closely with those of other federal departments and agencies and of other nations* (see pages 79–81).

■ *The new research and training programs at the National Institute of Environmental Health Sciences should be expanded, and the Institute should establish closer ties with EPA's health research program* (see pages 81–82).

■ *The Department of the Interior should develop a long-range plan for its environmental R&D activities and should work to integrate and focus its programs in the context of clearly defined goals* (see page 82).

■ *The National Park Service should establish a strong environmental research and monitoring program to build the knowledge base necessary to protect the resources of the National Park system* (see pages 82–83).

■ *The Bureau of Land Management should expand its environmental monitoring and technology programs and should seek the assistance of other federal agencies in devising land use, biological resources management, waste management, and monitoring programs to protect public lands and to ensure their productive use in the future* (see pages 83–84).

■ *The Department of Agriculture should continue to strengthen its environmental R&D by following the recommendations recently made by the National Research Council and the congressional Office of Technology Assessment that call for a substantial increase in funding for competitive research grants and for a more structured, integrated, and coordinated R&D planning system* (see pages 84–86).

- *The R&D activities of the Department of Energy National Laboratories should be evaluated to determine their potential to make future contributions to national and international environmental R&D programs* (see pages 86–89).

- *Department of Defense environment-related research and development efforts should be integrated with those of other federal departments and agencies. Alternatively, some of these activities could be transferred to environmental R&D programs within other departments and agencies* (see pages 89–90).

- *A larger proportion of the funds devoted to the cleanup of hazardous waste at federal facilities should be directed to research and development* (see pages 90–91).

LINKING AND COORDINATING PROGRAMS

The global nature of environmental problems requires that U.S. environmental R&D programs operate in concert with those of other nations. Furthermore, the federal environmental R&D effort will operate most effectively if it is closely linked with complementary programs in academia, nongovernmental organizations, and industry. Since the environmental R&D system should be more than the sum of its parts, more effective interactions between all parties engaged in environmental R&D should be promoted.

- **In order to strengthen the link between environmental R&D and policy development, assessment capabilities across federal agencies should be expanded. Furthermore, U.S. environmental R&D programs should be coupled more closely with those of other nations. Greater cooperation among scientific disciplines and among federal, nongovernmental, and industrial research programs should be encouraged** (see pages 92–97).

- *The linkages between environmental R&D and policy development should be strengthened, and the federal government should substantially increase its support of multidisciplinary policy studies and assessments designed to forge and evaluate these linkages.* The development of effective environmental policy requires interaction among the natural sciences, economics, political science, and law, as well as many other disciplines. To date, however, federal agencies have focused their environmental R&D efforts on the natural sciences: no single institution is responsible for pursuing funding authority to advance multidisciplinary research involving the social sciences. We recommend that the federal government devote a larger percentage of total environmental R&D dollars to policy research and assessment, including studies of the economic, social, legal, and political aspects of environmental problems from regional, national, and international perspectives.

■ *The United States should couple its environmental research and development efforts more closely with those of other nations.* International agencies, including the United Nations Environment Program and specialized agencies such as the World Meteorological Organization, as well as key nongovernmental scientific organizations, are promoting a range of international collaborative R&D efforts. World Health Organization programs like the International Program on Chemical Safety make important contributions to public health throughout the world. The United States should actively support programs of this kind. The United States should also collaborate with the European Community countries and with academic institutions abroad to develop and share new technologies. Collaborative relationships between the research institutions of various countries would be particularly worthwhile.

Other recommendations are discussed in more detail in the report:

■ *Communication and collaboration between the ecological and environmental health research communities should be enchanced in order to evaluate and address environmental problems in an integrated fashion* (see pages 97–99).

■ *The environmental research and policymaking linkages between federal agencies and nongovernmental organizations should be strengthened* (see pages 99–101).

■ *Environmental R&D programs within the federal government and industry should be linked more closely, and the federal government should continue to provide incentives for environmental R&D efforts in industry in order to advance common goals* (see pages 101–103).

BUILDING A STRONG INTELLECTUAL BASE

An improved R&D system will survive only if it is built on a strong foundation. Implicit in the recommendations above is the assumption that there must be a pool of highly trained professionals to carry out the research and development activities that are crucial to our environmental protection programs. There is a critical need for a continuing supply of well-trained professionals and state-of-the-art facilities and equipment to support their research efforts.

■ The science and technology base that underpins our environmental R&D programs must be strengthened to ensure the availability of environmental scientists and engineers, social scientists, and policy analysts, and to ensure adequate facilities and equipment to support their work (see pages 104–106).

■ *The National Science Foundation and other government agencies should take steps to strengthen the base upon which our national environmental R&D programs are built.* The scope and direction of grant programs in NSF and other agencies that support environmental R&D activities in universities, nongovernmental organizations, and elsewhere should be examined carefully to determine if additional funding is needed to support certain kinds of research activities. We believe that the NSF, in particular, should substantially expand extramural grants programs devoted to research designed to integrate the thinking across multiple disciplines, including policy research and assessment. NSF should pay particular attention to the adequacy of the nation's environmental science and technology disciplinary base. In addition, NSF, with the assistance of the National Research Council, should undertake a study of the future environmental R&D-related human resource needs of the nation.

■ *Both government and the private sector should take deliberate steps to improve educational programs in the environmental sciences.* Undergraduate biological, physical, engineering, business, and economics educational programs should include an environmental science component in their curricula. Graduate and postdoctoral training programs in the environmental and social sciences should be expanded.

THE WAY FORWARD

It is clear that wealth and physical resources alone will not be enough to solve the daunting environmental challenges we face. Advanced knowledge of earth's systems and processes is crucial, and developing it requires a strong federal effort in environmental R&D.

If adopted, our recommendations would aid in accomplishing several objectives, including a strengthening of the contribution of environmental R&D to the missions of federal departments and agencies. Monitoring and information storage would be improved, as would the government's ability to engage in assessment, strategic planning, and more effective environmental policy development. Better linkages among federal entities and with outside organizations will yield new knowledge, and investments in a strong science and technology base will help to ensure a continuing flow of high-quality environmental R&D.

Fundamentally, however, the federal government's environmental R&D effort suffers from weak leadership. It is a lack of direction, focus, and coordination that most limits the federal R&D enterprise. The United States has the ability to remain at the forefront of environmental R&D and consequently to meet the global environmental protection needs of the 21st century, but significant improvements must be made in our present system.

PART I
R&D FOR THE ENVIRONMENT

I

THE ENVIRONMENTAL CHALLENGES OF
TODAY AND TOMORROW

For most of those who watched the first moon landing in July 1969, two indelible images remain. The first is the television picture of the surface of the moon as Neil Armstrong stepped from the lunar lander. The second is the image of the surface of the earth, that breathtaking picture of our planet as seen from our closest celestial neighbor. The first image was a triumphal one, summarizing a decade of American technological achievements in space. But for many the second image was a warning.

At a time when public awareness of environmental problems was very much in its infancy, that image of our planet helped people to understand that the Earth is an integrated set of systems—landmasses, the atmosphere, oceans, the plant and animal kingdoms—and that a threat to one could harm them all. As one observer has written, "The image brought home as never before that our home is, after all, a planet—small, self-contained, and in some ways perhaps, fragile."[7]

In the more than twenty years since the nation first saw the images from the moon, scientific knowledge about the components of the earth's biosphere and the effects of human activity on them has increased, public concern has grown, and national, state, and local governments have enacted a wide range of environmental programs. As a result, progress has been made in some of the problem areas that first attracted widespread attention in the late 1960s. A 1991 report by the Organization for Economic Cooperation and Development (OECD) listed a number of achievements. These included reduction of urban air pollution by lead, sulfur dioxide, and particulate matter; reduced pollution of waterways by organic substances as a result of treatment of household and industrial wastewater; a decrease in the number of accidental oil spills; increases in the area of protected land and habitats; increased forest resources; better protection of a number of game species; a growing population of several threatened species; and reduction in the release into the environment of certain dangerous chemicals, such as DDT, PCBs, and mercury compounds.[8]

Some time after the 1972 Stockholm Conference on the Environment, however, a review by the United Nations Environment Program found that human interventions in natural systems had increased on a massive scale, and that there was an urgent need for remedial and preventive action. Those interventions had been accompanied by momentous advances in industrial activity and agricultural production and in human longevity and health.[9]

The past two decades have thus seen the persistence of some threats to the environment and the emergence of dangerous new ones. While there is less sulfur dioxide in the air in some cities, nitrogen oxides, urban smog, and fine particulates continue to be major problems. Growing concentrations of carbon dioxide and other greenhouse gases threaten to raise global temperatures. In the middle and late 1980s, the discovery of a thinning in the ozone layer over Antarctica led to the judgment that the earth's protective ozone layer is being depleted much more quickly in some regions than had been thought. About 27 million acres of tropical forest are estimated to be disappearing each year, taking with them a wealth of biological diversity that can never be replaced. Groundwaters, once thought to be invulnerable to contamination, have deteriorated because of salinization and pollution from urban runoff, pesticides, and seepage from contaminated industrial sites. Soil continues to be degraded by erosion and pollution from a wide range of sources, and development is putting pressure on critical environmental areas such as coastal regions and wetlands, farmland, and natural preserves. Many areas are becoming more vulnerable to extreme events such as droughts and floods. In short, our planet is still very much in danger.

PEOPLE AND GLOBAL ENVIRONMENTAL CHANGE

Although each of these problems has unique characteristics, all have a common cause—the actions of humans. The earth's environment has experienced dramatic changes in its five-billion-year history, but most have resulted from natural events: the movement of continents and oceans, the coming and going of ice ages, changes in the magnetic orientation of the earth, the evolution and extinction of plant and animal species. These natural forces continue to work today, but as a recent National Research Council study stressed: "The earth has entered a period of hydrological, climatological, and biological change that differs from previous episodes of global change in the extent to which it is human in origin. Humans have always sought to transform their surroundings. But, for the first time, they have begun to play a central role in altering global biogeochemical systems and the earth as a whole."[10]

POPULATION GROWTH AND INCREASING CONSUMER DEMAND

Human population growth and increased and more diverse consumer demand are the chief driving forces for this stress on the biosphere. Population growth has been dramatic. Human population did not reach the one billion mark until about 1830. It reached two billion in the 1930s, four billion in 1975, and will probably reach six billion in 1997. The rate of future growth and the times at which population may be expected to stabilize vary greatly from region to region and are determined by social and economic factors that affect development in each country. With current growth rates, world population would double again in 40 years, but the doubling figure may come much sooner or later, depending upon policies adopted in the meantime.[11]

More people consume more resources. Although technological advance can help alleviate the stresses imposed by population growth, technical fixes and economic expansion alone cannot be relied on to solve the population problem.[12]

But population growth *per se* is only part of the problem. The quantity and diversity of goods consumed by many of the earth's people have been rising. While this means that some people are better off, many of the processes that raise living standards deplete the vital resources—soils, forests, species, water—on which future populations depend. Thus, while population growth is slowing in wealthier countries, these nations continue to use more energy and other natural resources and produce more contaminants than do developing nations.

The combination of population growth and rising consumer demand has particularly ominous implications for the future. The people in poorer nations want and deserve living standards more like those of the developed world. However, the challenge is to raise their living standards without further damaging the environment and making them more vulnerable to natural disaster. As William Ruckelshaus has warned, "If the four-fifths of humanity now in developing nations attempt to create wealth using the methods of the past, at some point the result will be unacceptable world ecological damage."[13]

SCALE OF ENVIRONMENTAL DAMAGE

The scale of environmental damage has also increased dramatically. Human-induced environmental damage was once characterized by local episodes of pollution that were confined to discrete geographical areas. Now cause and effect often lie in different parts of the globe. For example, pollutant emissions from factories in one part of the globe may cause acid rain half a continent or more away. Introducing irrigated farming in one part of the world may reduce the productivity of marine fisheries elsewhere by altering water quality and flow patterns through damming or consumption. The use of chlorofluorocarbons (CFCs) in the developed world affects the atmosphere for people on every continent.

The need to address environmental problems in the context of local communities, each with its distinctive combination of resources and people, is becoming more and more urgent. Significant environmental degradation is taking place over decades and years, not centuries. Moreover, the actions of humans today can have effects far into the future that will be difficult to reverse in the short run. Some, such as the extinction of species, are irreversible. Because environmental systems are operating closer to their limits, the problems are likely to occur sooner, and systems are likely to take longer to recover. For example, the CFCs we emit today will continue to deplete stratospheric ozone for decades, and arresting the growth of emissions of greenhouse gases still leaves us with the possibility of global climate change for years into the future.

ECONOMIC BENEFITS, ENVIRONMENTAL COSTS

The pressing and widespread threats to the biosphere appear more closely linked with the functioning of the world economy than ever before. Today's global economy has reinforced the geographic separation of resource extraction, production, and consumption. Hence, those who reap the economic benefits of using natural resources are often different from those who bear the environmental costs. This complex of issues was brought into sharper focus by the preparations for the United Nations Conference on Environment and Development in Rio de Janeiro in June 1992 and by the conference itself. This new awareness led to an international agenda for research on environment and development and various nonbinding agreements, but much more must be done to stem global environmental degradation.

THE KEY ROLE OF ENVIRONMENTAL R&D

The nation will be able to deal much more effectively with environmental problems once they are better understood. Our ability to understand earth processes and human dynamics is determined by what research is conducted, how it is organized, and how well it is assessed and presented in establishing and implementing environmental policy. And our ability to identify, control, prevent, and clean up pollutants is limited by the effectiveness of the technologies we develop and our ingenuity in finding sound means of promoting the widespread adoption of those technologies. Environmental problems pose a special challenge to the world's scientific and engineering communities, one that evokes the image of the first human steps on the moon: Can scientists and engineers generate the kind of large-scale and highly focused effort that took us into space and apply it to developing the understanding necessary to protect our global environment?

S&T AS SOURCES OF INNOVATION

We believe that our ability to respond to the environmental and economic challenges of today and tomorrow is strongly dependent on the information produced by a well-organized and productive federal research and development system. But we also recognize that protecting the environment will require a new and more effective application of scientific and technological skills. Many of the accomplishments of science and technology that have helped achieve a higher standard of living in the past have been geared to using more and more resources to produce more and more goods and services.

As Congressman George E. Brown, Jr., recently described the problem: "If we embrace the belief in science and technology as the great contributors to progress, then are we also embracing resource depletion, environmental degradation, and economic disparity in the name of this progress?" He points out that the solution is to "begin to think of science and technology in entirely different terms—not as mechanisms to increase our wealth and comfort through exploitation of material resources, but as sources of innovation that can drive us to less consumption, less pollution, less depletion of resources, and lower rates of population growth."[14]

Technology has already allowed us to use resources more efficiently, but meeting the future demands of both developing and developed countries will require new technologies that are highly efficient and that result in little or no waste (see Box 1).

NATURAL AND SOCIAL SCIENCES

Meeting the challenges of the future requires research in both the natural and social sciences, as well as multidisciplinary studies that cut across fields of science. A major research goal in the natural sciences, for example, is to advance our knowledge of earth systems so that environmental processes can be better modeled. This will require sophisticated technology, including space-based and earth-based observation systems to collect data and to verify model predictions, and information management systems to maintain comprehensive databases. Advances in the biomedical sciences will cast light on the susceptibilities of humans to environmental risks. More knowledge of the basic mechanisms of initiation, promotion, and prevention of diseases and disorders will allow us to anticipate, and respond to, environmental health threats. Similarly, advances in all areas of environmental engineering, earth systems, and social sciences are needed in order to identify and develop new pollution prevention techniques and to promote mitigation measures.

Perhaps most important, a wide range of research advances will be needed if "sustainable development" is to be achieved—growth that is a product of efficient consumption of energy and materials, minimizing waste and maximizing recycling, stabilizing land use, and ensuring that no damage is done to the future environment on which further growth depends.

Society, however, cannot apply a quick technological fix to every environmental problem it encounters. The social sciences have a vital role to play in understanding how human activities influence the physical, chemical, and biological processes of the earth system and in devising means of changing patterns of human behavior. Finding more effective ways to promote stable population is especially important. Since environmental degra-

---

Box 1. Low-Waste/No-Waste Technologies—the Key to Attaining Global Environmental Goals

---

If global environmental goals are to be attained, governmental policies must encourage development of low-waste/no-waste technologies. The efforts of the Du Pont Company provide one example of the potential of American industry to promote environmentally benign technologies. Du Pont invented nylon and has produced it in the United States for more than 50 years. The processes by which the final product as well as the major intermediate compounds are made have been improved continually in terms of yield, quality, and waste minimization. Currently, two U.S. plants make the primary intermediate compounds through essentially identical processes, resulting in the same yield and quality characteristics and about the same waste generation and emission.

A new, advanced plant is now being built by Du Pont in Singapore to produce the key nylon intermediate, adipic acid. It will use the same process, based on cyclohexane technology, as the two U.S. plants. The process has, however, been improved so that there is a higher yield of product, less consumption of energy, and considerably less waste generated (about 20 percent less waste water alone); air emissions have also been reduced, by 97 to 99 percent. A material that was formerly waste has also been turned into a beneficial product for commercial sale. Greenhouse gases, now emitted from the plants in the United States, will be reclaimed or destroyed, and not released to the atmosphere. Overall, the Singapore plant will be less energy-intensive and much more environmentally friendly than the existing plants.

Du Pont's next-generation adipic acid plant is being planned for Europe, where the company plans to use a step change in technology that will bring further improvements to the product and reduce the potential environmental load from the plant even more than the Singapore plant. This technology will achieve considerable reductions in air and water emissions, and by-products will be converted back to feedstock and recycled into the process. No oxides of nitrogen or waste water will be released into the environment. Commercialization of this facility is expected within the next 4 to 6 years. After the new technologies have been proven in commercial operations, the process and environmental improvements in both the Singapore and European plants will be considered for retrofitting into the U.S. plants.

---

dation is closely linked with industrialization, we must explore ways to harness economic forces to work for environmental protection, not against it.

GLOBAL EFFORT NEEDED

Ultimately, ensuring that our planet will sustain the human family in perpetuity will take a global effort with keen sensitivity to geographic diversity. The importance of international collaboration in environmental R&D is underscored by the past record of research accomplishments. U.S. R&D efforts in many areas have been influenced strongly by the accomplishments of scientists and engineers in other nations. For example, much of the original research on major environmental problems, such as acid rain and global climate change, was done by investigators in Europe and Scandinavia.[15] The United States, as a major source of scientific and technological know-how, will have to play a leading role, in concert with other major developed countries.

GOALS AND PRIORITIES

Finally, it is important to articulate our environmental goals clearly and to set well-defined priorities. To achieve a sustainable society, we must have a clear understanding of our environmental objectives and a strategy for achieving them. This is especially true at a time when both developing and developed countries are faced with major economic challenges. Since not all environmental problems can be solved at once, we must determine which are the most important. A close linkage between the needs of policymakers and the research enterprise is essential for this purpose.

AN EFFECTIVE FEDERAL ENVIRONMENTAL R&D PROGRAM

As a nation, we face enormous environmental challenges, and strong and effective federal R&D programs are a prerequisite to attacking these problems successfully and, in doing so, providing hope and a means of action for today's generation and those of the future. As the chapters that follow will show, the existing federal R&D structure was constructed for a time and set of issues that no longer correspond to today's demands. An examination and rethinking of the federal government's environmental R&D effort is essential in order to ensure the scientific resources and leadership that a national and global environmental protection effort requires.

THE PRESENT R&D SYSTEM:
WHY IMPROVEMENTS ARE NECESSARY

R&D MISSIONS OF THE MAJOR DEPARTMENTS AND AGENCIES

Although the definition of *environmental R&D* can vary widely, we define it as research and development directed to maintaining environmental quality, including monitoring, testing, evaluation, prevention, mitigation, assessment, and policy analysis. This definition includes

- Investigations designed to understand the structure and function of the biosphere and the impact that human activities have on it
- Research to understand the conditions necessary to support human existence without destroying the resource base
- Research to define the properties and adverse effects of toxic substances on human health and the environment
- The development of technologies to monitor pollutants and their impacts

■ The development of pollution-control technologies
■ The economic and social research directed at understanding the many complex, interrelated factors that influence environmental quality[16]

Using this definition, we examined federal R&D programs in the natural and physical sciences devoted to understanding both the pristine and degraded states of our air, land, water, and biological resources. We also considered programs directed at understanding the impacts of pollution on public health, as well as social science activities focusing on the human causes of and responses to resource depletion and environmental change. Much environmental R&D is not directly related to the impacts of pollution. A large proportion of the federal effort is devoted to understanding earth systems, including air, land, and ocean resources. Understanding these systems is critical to national and global environmental protection efforts.

Many federal agencies support environment-related research and development. The federal government spent more than $5 billion on environmental R&D in fiscal year 1992. The bulk of this research was in the environmental sciences ($3.6 billion) and engineering ($1.1 billion) areas; information sciences ($195 million) and work in the social sciences ($40 million) made up the remainder (see Figure 1). Table 1 shows estimated federal support for environmental R&D by field of science, and Table 2 shows funding for environmental R&D by department and agency.

Major environmental research programs support the missions of numerous federal departments and agencies, including the Environmental Protection Agency, the National Science Foundation, the National Oceanic and Atmospheric Administration, the National Aeronautics and Space Administration, and the Departments of Energy, the Interior, Health and Human Services, Agriculture, and Defense.[17] The activities of these departments and agencies are described in Appendix A and are summarized in Box 2 (page 40), and it is on the programs of these agencies that our analysis focuses.

IMPROVING THE FEDERAL R&D EFFORT

At first glance, the federal environmental research and development effort seems impressive. More than a dozen federal departments and agencies conduct environment-related R&D, and total annual federal funding is more than $5 billion. Unfortunately, the scope, quality, and organization of this effort are unequal to the increasingly complex challenges to environmental R&D that we outlined earlier.

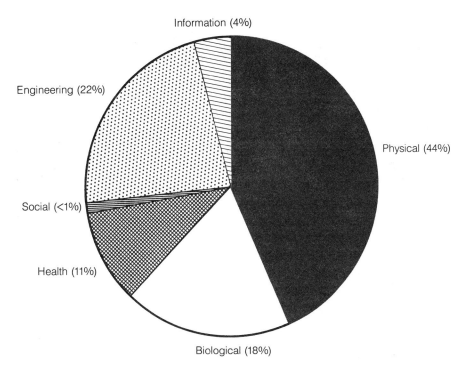

Figure 1. 1992 Federal Environmental R&D Expenditure, by Field of Science

Table 1. Estimated Federal Funding for Environmental R&D, by Field of Science ($ billions, Fiscal Year 1992)

Environmental sciences	3.6
Physical	2.2
Biological	0.9
Health	0.5
Engineering	1.1
Information sciences	0.2
Social sciences	<0.1[a]
	5.0[b]

[a] Approximately $40 million.
[b] Total reflects rounding.

Source: Based on an analysis by Kathleen Gramp, Albert H. Teich, and Stephen D. Nelson, American Association for the Advancement of Science, "Federal Funding of Environmental R&D," a report to the National Academy of Sciences and the Carnegie Commission on Science, Technology, and Government.

Table 2. Estimated Federal Funding for Environmental R&D by Agency ($ million, Fiscal Year 1992)

Environmental Protection Agency	502
National Oceanic and Atmospheric Administration	319
National Science Foundation	541
Department of Health and Human Services	
National Institute of Environmental Health Sciences (NIEHS)	303[a]
National Institute of Occupational Safety & Health (NIOSH)	93
Agency for Toxic Substances and Disease Registry (ATSDR)	55[b]
National Center for Toxicological Research (NCTR)	3[c]
Department of the Interior	
U.S. Geological Survey	367
Fish and Wildlife Service	85
Other	72
Department of Agriculture	
Agricultural Research Service	162
Cooperative State Research Service	119
Forest Service	115
Other	7
Department of Energy	799
Department of Defense	577
Department of Transportation	17
National Aeronautics and Space Administration	826
Smithsonian Institution	33
Agency for International Development	45
Tennessee Valley Authority	31
TOTAL	5,071

[a] Includes $51 million transferred under Superfund from EPA to NIEHS.
[b] Funds are transferred to ATSDR from EPA through Superfund program.
[c] The entire NCTR budget is about $30 million. An estimated 10 percent of the center's budget is devoted to environment-related R&D.

Source: Based on an analysis by Kathleen Gramp, Albert H. Teich, and Stephen D. Nelson, American Association for the Advancement of Science, "Federal Funding of Environmental R&D," a report to the National Academy of Sciences and the Carnegie Commission on Science, Technology, and Government.

      Our present environmental R&D system is the product of its origins and so is organized to deal with the simpler issues of the past. It began as a series of individual research programs that were undertaken in response to specific problems such as urban smog and the pollution of lakes and rivers. The first programs tended, therefore, to be short-term and crisis-oriented, focusing on mitigating dangers to the public health. In the 1970s and 1980s, for example, much of our attention was devoted to hazard identification: many chemicals had been used in commerce since the 1940s, but we knew little or nothing about their effects on human health or the environment.

Over the years, many federal laboratories were established in response to specific environmental concerns. Today, however, these laboratories do not meet the nation's needs. D. Allan Bromley, Assistant to the President for Science and Technology, recently described the need to rethink the missions of federal research laboratories

> There are over 700 federal laboratories, and we invest over $20 billion a year in them. They embrace an astonishing breadth and depth of science and technology, including some of the best science and technology to be found anywhere in the world. Many of these laboratories were established in the immediate post-World War II period, and they originally had very specific missions and objectives. Many of these original missions were satisfied years ago, so that the laboratories are having to adjust their programs to remain in close touch with evolving national needs. As components of the federal R&D enterprise, federal laboratories engaging in environmental R&D must redefine their missions in the context of evolving national needs.[18]

WEAKNESSES OF THE PRESENT SYSTEM

Ten or twenty years ago, questions about whether current land and water use could be maintained in the foreseeable future received relatively little attention. A "catch up, clean up" approach dominated the environmental protection agenda. Little attention was paid to developing an integrated, forward-looking R&D system that would identify trends, anticipate problems, and address root causes instead of symptoms.[19]

As a result, two decades later our R&D system remains diffuse, reactive, and focused on short-range, end-of-the-pipe solutions. Mechanisms to coordinate and integrate the products of environmental research conducted by federal, state, academic, and nongovernmental institutions are weak. Until recently, pollution reduction and prevention have received relatively little attention. We have difficulty developing the comprehensive information necessary to evaluate the state of the environment, the subtle ways in which it is changing, and the opportunities to help human populations become more resilient. Limitations in our ability to coordinate, assess, and disseminate research information hamper the public and private sectors' efforts to attack environmental problems. Finally, research to date on the international aspects of environmental conditions has received a relatively low priority in the federal government.[20] A number of organizations, such as Resources for the Future and the World Resources Institute, have invested in international research on the social and ecological consequences of U.S. environmental policy, but relatively little has been done directly by federal agencies.

Box 2. R&D Missions of the Major Departments and Agencies

More than twenty governmental organizations house R&D programs related to environmental quality. Specific environmental research programs support the missions of nine major federal departments and agencies.* Depending on how broadly one defines "environment," the federal government spent nearly $5 billion on environmental R&D in fiscal year 1992. In the descriptions that follow, the budget figures for particular years refer to fiscal years.

Environmental Protection Agency. The EPA has a strong applied research program and is the *de facto* "lead agency" for environmental R&D, overseeing several programs that comprise the largest internal environmental research effort in the federal government. Regulation has been its dominant concern. The agency operates its research programs within the Office of Research and Development (ORD). ORD's eight offices and twelve laboratories had a 1992 budget of $502 million. ORD's Office of Exploratory Research coordinates a small extramural program in basic, long-term research. EPA has traditionally devoted a small proportion of its resources to basic research. In real dollars, EPA's R&D budget declined by about 11 percent between 1980 and 1992.

National Science Foundation. The National Science Foundation (NSF) supports basic scientific and engineering research, education, and training in the environmental field through competitive grant programs. Two major divisions, covering a wide range of disciplines, funded research totaling more than $540 million in 1992, making NSF the largest source of extramural grants in the environmental field. The major directorates of NSF fund research in biotic systems and resources, biosciences, geoscience, and the anthropogenic causes and effects of ecological change. This funding supports research at the National Center for Atmospheric Research and a number of oceanographic centers.

National Oceanic and Atmospheric Administration. The National Oceanic and Atmospheric Administration (NOAA), within the Department of Commerce, maintains an environmental research program that focuses on oceanic and atmospheric technology. The program includes work in applied weather research, water quality and coastal ecosystem management, marine life, and global climate change. Some $319 million was spent in 1992 for environment-related research at NOAA, an increase of more than 50 percent over the $216 million appropriated just three years ago. (This figure does not include $265 million to support the National Environment Satellite, Data, and Information Service.)

Department of Energy. The Department of Energy (DOE) operates a program in Biological and Environmental Research that aims to identify, understand, and anticipate the long-term health and environmental consequences of energy use. Many of the key programs are carried out through the Office of Energy Research and the Fossil Energy Division; also involved are the National Environmental Research Parks and the National Labora-

Box 2. (continued)

tories system. DOE spent nearly $800 million on environmental R&D in 1992. DOE plans to devote tremendous resources to the cleanup of waste generated at federal facilities engaged in weapons research. However, only a small proportion of these resources can be classified as R&D.

Department of the Interior. The bulk of environmental R&D at the Department of the Interior (DOI) is located in three of the department's five divisions, with the largest programs at the U.S. Geological Survey ($367 million in 1992), and the Fish and Wildlife Service ($85 million). USGS conducts research to gather, classify, and analyze information on land, water, mineral and energy resources; FWS manages the nation's fish and wildlife resources and conducts research through a system of National Research Centers and Cooperative Research Units. Small programs exist in the National Park Service, the Minerals Management Service, the Bureau of Mines, the Bureau of Land Management, and in other units, including the Bureau of Reclamation.

National Aeronautics and Space Administration. NASA's environment-related R&D is largely devoted to monitoring changes in land surface, oceans, and atmosphere through space-based observations. Through its Earth Observing System (EOS) program, NASA coordinates international efforts to monitor global change. NASA devoted $826 million to environment-related research programs in 1992.

Department of Health and Human Services. The focal point for government research in the environmental health field is the National Institute of Environmental Health Sciences (NIEHS) within the National Institutes of Health. NIEHS supports several university-based Environmental Health Science Centers and supports pre- and post-doctoral training in environmental health sciences. Research funding at NIEHS in 1992 was $303 million. Like other NIH institutes, it sponsors a large extramural grants program.

The National Institute of Occupational Safety and Health (NIOSH), the Center for Environmental Health and Injury Control (CEHIC), and the Agency for Toxic Substances and Disease Registry (ATSDR) also engage in environmental health research. ATSDR is responsible for conducting applied research on the health effects of exposure to hazardous substances, while CEHIC engages in basic toxicology research. NIOSH's mission is to conduct research to ensure safe and healthful working conditions.† In 1992, $93 million was spent on research at NIOSH. In addition, the National Center for Toxicological Research (NCTR), located within the Food and Drug Administration, conducts research on food contaminants and is working to advance risk assessment methodologies.

Department of Agriculture. The U.S. Department of Agriculture (USDA) houses the majority of its environment-related research in three program areas: the U.S. Forest Service (USFS), the Agricultural Research Service (ARS), and the Cooperative State Research Service. For fiscal year 1992, the Forest Service research program focuses on "national problem" areas,

---

Box 2. *(continued)*

---

including tropical forestry, recycling, and the ecological and social values of forest land. The Forest Service's 1992 R&D budget was about $115 million. Soil erosion, irrigation, and pesticides and fertilizer studies constitute the bulk of the research program of the Agricultural Research Service. Funding for the ARS was $162 million in 1992. The Cooperative State Research Service budget was $119 million.

Department of Defense.   All three branches of the military in the Department of Defense (DOD) have programs in environmental R&D. The largest of these efforts is in the Office of Naval Research (ONR) in the Department of the Navy. The U.S. Army Corps of Engineers has an active wetlands study program and coordinates the Strategic Environmental Resources and Development Program. Research at DoD is divided into two major categories: the natural environment and environmental quality. The budget for environmental R&D within DoD was $577 million in 1992.

Smithsonian Institution.   Though relatively small, with a budget in FY 1992 of $33 million, the Smithsonian's environmental R&D effort covers a wide range of areas, including biodiversity, ecology, conservation, and the history of the interaction between people and nature.

Other Agencies.   Small environmental R&D programs are also found at the Agency for International Development, the Tennessee Valley Authority, and the Department of Transportation.

---

* For a detailed discussion see Steven J. Kafka.[16]
† NIOSH FY1992 Budget Justification, p. 487.

Insufficient resources are devoted to environmental biology, and there is a need for more interdisciplinary studies. Most ecological processes are inadequately understood, and several organizations have recommended increased federal funding in this area. Geographical studies of the interrelation of land, water, and biota in landscapes and regions are conspicuously weak. At both regional and local scales, economic, social, and political studies of environmental issues must be better integrated with studies in the natural sciences.[21]

TECHNOLOGY DEVELOPMENT

In discussing these issues, it is important to emphasize the "D" of environmental R&D—that is, technology development as separate from scientific inquiry. While research into the fundamental causes and processes of environmental problems is crucial, equally important is the technological research undertaken to develop methods of avoiding or mitigating environmental impacts. In other words, technology development seeks to offer solutions to the environmental problems that environmental research has uncovered and analyzed.

COSTS AND BENEFITS OF TECHNOLOGY

Historically, more advanced technology has often had detrimental environmental impacts; witness the widespread use of fossil fuels with the advent of the industrial age, the development of synthetic materials and their toxic by-products, or the soil erosion that accompanies more mechanically intensive farming practices. Technology development need not result in more pollution, however; on the contrary, technologies today are central to our efforts to protect the environment. The most promising areas for realizing the gains of environmental technology today relate to energy use and the development of alternative fuels, to agricultural practices that use less harmful pesticides developed through biotechnology, and to the reduction and prevention of pollution in industrial production processes.

INDUSTRY ROLE

Private industry is a major player in environmental R&D, particularly in applied research on environmental technologies. It is estimated that private industry funds more than half of all the R&D in the nation and that it conducts another 20 percent of the total through government contracts. In all, private industry is responsible for more than 70 percent of all R&D in the United States.[22] And although it is difficult to pinpoint exactly how much privately funded research is related to the environment, a recent report by the World Resources Institute on environmentally critical technology states that up to half of industry R&D budgets is directed toward environmental technology R&D.[23]

For quite some time, industry's efforts in environmental R&D were limited to developing technologies and processes aimed at meeting the requirements of environmental regulations. Today, however, industry's focus on environmental concerns results not only from the need to meet governmental standards; an even greater incentive is the potential for seizing new business opportunities and realizing economic gains. Industry is moving quickly to develop environmentally sound technologies that will use energy more efficiently and generate less waste, leading in turn to lower production and disposal costs. The potential market for new and emerging technologies in air pollution control, composite materials, nonfossil fuels, bioengineering, and other fields is large, and industry is racing to capture it through its environmental technology R&D efforts. "Environmentally friendly" has become a powerful marketing tool as well, as producers aim to attract consumers with products that have less harmful impacts on the environment.

FEDERAL ROLE IN INDUSTRIAL TECHNOLOGY

Technology development was originally thought to be exclusively in the private sector's domain. But beginning with technological research in defense, space, and energy, a consensus has developed that government does have a role in promoting technology development, primarily at the precompetitive stage or the stage at which knowledge is nonproprietary and broadly applicable.[24] Technology is recognized as vital to economic development, and so is intricately wrapped up in public policy considerations. The 1988 Omnibus Trade and Competitiveness Act committed the government to supporting technology development that is "essential for long-term security and economic prosperity." Today it is becoming clear that environmental technologies fit this description.

The federal government is involved in promoting industrial efforts in environmental R&D in several ways. Besides the direct federal funding of R&D through contracts, the government also promotes industrial efforts in environmental R&D through economic incentives. A 20 percent tax credit for increments to R&D, enacted in 1981, aims to encourage R&D by reducing the overall cost of R&D by up to 4 percent. The National Cooperative Research Act of 1984 allows private companies to form research alliances without facing antitrust allegations.

The government is also a major purchaser of industrial products. Government procurement policies and specifications can have a significant impact on industrial programs. The Carnegie Commission's report *Technology and Economic Performance* cited the need for government to provide incentives for private-sector R&D through a stable regulatory environment to decrease investment risk and uncertainty, and through opportunities for the commercialization of technologies developed under government contract.[25]

PUBLIC–PRIVATE PARTNERSHIP

The idea of a more explicit public–private partnership in environmental R&D is only beginning to take shape. The National Environmental Technology Applications Corporation (NETAC) is an example of such a partnership. Established in 1988, NETAC is a nonprofit consulting company set up through a cooperative agreement with EPA to focus on environmental technology commercialization. NETAC has programs directed at the evaluation of new technologies, international technology transfer, and technology development, demonstration, and evaluation, among others. It works to combine a private-sector profit orientation with a thorough understanding of the demands and goals of government regulation. We believe that this kind of partnership, focused on the needs of both the public and private sectors, is a step in the right direction.

U.S. TECHNOLOGY POLICY AND THE ENVIRONMENT

Despite the growing importance of environmental R&D in private industry and the undeniable connections between technology development and economic health, to date there has been little prominence given to environmental issues in U.S. technology policy. While other nations around the world support technological development as a way of solving national economic problems, some devoting entire government departments to issues of technology, the United States lacks even a "comprehensive coordinating mechanism within the Federal government to evaluate the Federal effort in developing technology."[26] The lack of Federal support in basic technology development and the lack of a long-term technology policy led the World Resources Institute to conclude that the "need for the new technology to solve the environmental problems has been inadequately recognized and that the government's role in encouraging such technologies is underdeveloped."[27]

MATCHING RESOURCES WITH PROBLEMS

Environmental protection efforts are expensive, and at a time of intense international economic competition and growing federal deficits, it is important to match resources carefully with problems. Over the past twenty years, the United States (combined government and private efforts) has spent close to $1 trillion on pollution control. It is estimated that environmental regulations imposed additional costs totaling $109 billion in 1992, and that these costs will increase to $184 billion annually by 2000.[28] The economic benefits are more difficult to quantify but may exceed the costs by a large margin.

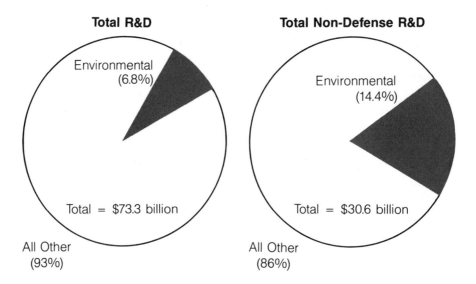

Figure 2. Federal Environmental R&D Spending vs. All Other Federal R&D Spending (1992)

Although regulatory costs are very large, the federal environmental R&D effort represents just 7 percent of total government R&D expenditures and 14 percent of total nondefense R&D expenditures (see Figure 2). With a budget deficit estimated at about $300 billion for fiscal year 1992, and large deficits expected in future years, the federal government will be constrained in its ability to address environmental needs. As in the past, federal funding for environmental protection is not likely to keep pace with environmental problems and the expense of addressing them.[29] However, if we are to attain the goal of reducing environmental regulatory costs while simultaneously improving environmental quality and addressing emerging problems, a robust environmental R&D effort is essential—one that carefully directs expenditures so that they yield maximum returns.

ORGANIZATIONAL CONSIDERATIONS

The structure and function of federal R&D programs are largely determined by the organization and mission of the federal departments and agencies they support. The federal environmental R&D infrastructure is shown in Figure 3. Federal agencies and departments cannot carry out their missions without the scientific and technological foundation created by research and development. Clearly, federal R&D programs must be organized in such

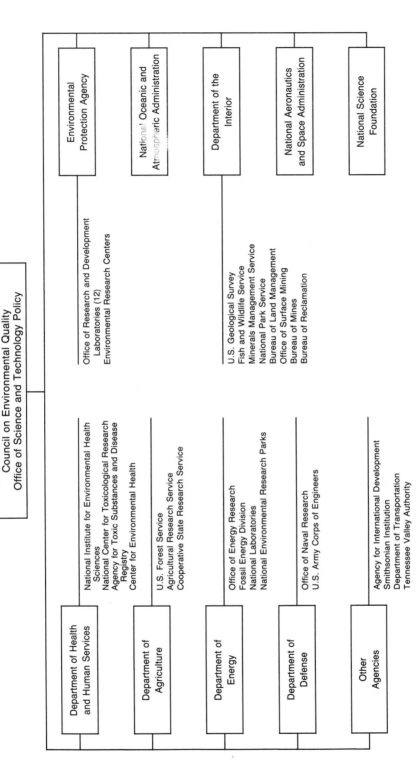

Figure 3. Current Federal Environmental R&D Infrastructure

a way that this fundamental requirement can be met. We do not believe, however, that a mere rearrangement of existing agencies and programs will solve the problem of directing environmental R&D toward its new and larger challenges. To be sure, reorganization may improve the management of current programs. But it is precisely this intimate — and necessary — connection with existing agency missions that most inhibits environmental R&D in tracking new problems.

Thus, while we take as given that environmental R&D should continue to support existing agency missions, we have been guided by other, broader principles in developing our recommendations — a capability to conduct strategic planning, to anticipate future R&D needs, and to undertake policy analyses; effective monitoring, information storage, and assessment capabilities; a strong science and technology base; and effective linkages with other federal and international programs. The key to achieving all of these objectives is leadership, particularly at the White House level. We discuss these principles briefly before moving on to our recommendations.

STRUCTURAL FRAGMENTATION

Structural fragmentation of environmental R&D hampers the strategic planning and policy coordination needed to establish and attain environmental goals. This problem is highlighted by the few instances in which it has been successfully addressed. For example, the Federal Coordinating Council on Science, Engineering, and Technology (FCCSET), administered through the White House Office of Science and Technology Policy, has played a key role in coordinating U.S. research efforts in global climate change. FCCSET oversees the U.S. Global Change Research Program, a $1.3 billion research effort involving eleven major departments and agencies (see Box 3). The task is daunting, but FCCSET has been successful in bringing together many diverse programs and agencies in an effort to understand and attack one of the more complex global environmental problems facing us.

In general, strategic planning and policy coordination remain a problem. There is no focal point for setting broad environmental policy for all federal agencies. It is important to note that EPA in particular is not such a focal point at present. Although EPA is the leader in implementing laws and regulatory policies, its research program is not now the centerpiece of the federal environmental R&D system, and its current programs devote little attention to sustainable development. Furthermore, although FCCSET is a useful mechanism for coordinating agency research programs, it is less useful for setting new research goals.

Box 3.   U.S. Global Change Research Program

The Federal Coordinating Council on Science, Engineering, and Technology (FCCSET), through its Committee on Earth Sciences (CES) established the U.S. Global Change Research Program (USGCRP) in 1989. Beginning with funding of $134 million in FY89, USGCRP has grown to $1.3 billion in 1992. The space- and ground-based observation and assessment capabilities are provided by a large number of federal agencies. Contributors to the focused research program include NASA, NSF, NOAA, DOE, USDA, DOI, and EPA. The Defense Department participates as well. Representatives from the Council on Environmental Quality, the Departments of State and Transportation, the Office of Management and Budget, and the White House offices of Science and Technology Policy and of Policy Development help provide executive oversight in addition to the participatory agencies.

The primary objectives of the research program are to

- Document the global earth system
- Study the physical, geological, chemical, biological, and social processes of the earth system
- Develop models of this system for predicting future trends and impacts

Research priorities include studies of greenhouse gases, ozone depletion, agriculture and ecosystems, and water policy. The goal of the program is to develop a scientific understanding of these phenomena and their potential impacts on human health and the environment.

LACK OF COORDINATION: CONSEQUENCES AND COSTS

Without a central coordinating mechanism, it is also difficult to establish budget priorities, conduct research efficiently and effectively, and then communicate the resulting data to those who can assess it and mold it into policy. For example, it took a multiagency panel, the National Acid Precipitation Assessment Program, more than ten years to address the many associated problems of acid rain, and the results of the project provided only weak guidance for policy directions.[30] Convening a multiagency panel for each potential issue is not an efficient way of establishing a coordinating mechanism to address environmental problems.

One consequence of a fragmented federal environmental R&D system is the difficulty of obtaining timely and useful information. Relatively new environmental concerns such as acid rain and stratospheric ozone depletion have brought to light the need to improve environmental monitoring and statistical capabilities at the federal level. Without a system for compiling, analyzing, and disseminating the massive amounts of statistical information generated by existing monitoring and research efforts, important data and findings are at risk of being used inappropriately, or being overlooked altogether.

The capacity both to meet regulatory needs and to provide data and information for basic research requires a strong environmental statistical and monitoring capacity. A new economic statistic is published in the U.S. virtually every day, and $1.9 billion was spent in 1989 to maintain this information system.[31] Comparatively little broad statistical information is readily available in the environmental field, despite the fact that environmental trends can strongly influence public policies and may have an impact on our everyday lives.

CHANGING PROBLEMS, DIFFERENT RESPONSES

In assessing the scientific and technological base that undergirds environmental R&D programs, it is important to keep in mind the changing characteristics of environmental issues. The problems of today demand a more complex, coordinated, and flexible R&D structure than did those of twenty years ago. More disciplines must be recruited to the effort. In addition, just as our perspective must be broadened from a local to a national and ultimately to an international one, environmental R&D must also be expanded beyond the traditional natural and physical science disciplines. Environmental policy requires more than an understanding of the ecological and health effects of particular actions and pollutants; it demands an understanding of the effects of changes in population and consumption patterns, of the potential economic and social implications, and of the two-way interactions between human activities and environmental quality.

Of particular importance in this regard, federal environmental R&D programs must provide a solid scientific foundation for making environmental policy decisions based on risk assessment. The public perception of problems and the political process for addressing them may sometimes deflect attention from what are truly the greatest threats to human health or the environment. Effectively combining public perceptions of risk and scientific assessments of risk can lead to better policy and enhanced environmental and health quality. In order to determine which problems pose the greatest risk, however, the resources must be in place to identify and respond to scientifically determined risk. The ability of scientists, policymakers, and others to communicate information on health hazards and help the public understand environmental problems is an equally important part of the process.

Environmental research must be broadened and linkages established in other ways, too. Many of the existing research programs focus on treating symptoms. There is a need to enhance and link basic, long-term research with the applied research of the regulatory agencies. An understanding of environmental processes and technologies can allow problems to be addressed at their source and perhaps mitigated or eliminated before they require remedial actions. Also, the federal R&D effort must take into account the variability of geographical regions of the United States. As the EPA's *Unfinished Business* report recognizes, national priorities do not necessarily reflect local situations. Analysis of problems on the local level is necessary for setting environmental research and protection goals and priorities.[32]

LINKS WITH OTHER NATIONS AND OTHER INSTITUTIONS

Aside from the need to coordinate research and policy internally, federal environmental R&D programs would benefit from stronger ties to nongovernmental organizations (NGOs), universities, and industries.[33] Researchers in these institutions, both in the United States and in foreign countries, often conduct the most forward-looking, cutting-edge research, but their work is often not well integrated into the policymaking process. And, because of the increasingly global nature of environmental issues, the federal research effort should create and support mechanisms that will connect U.S. scientists and engineers with those of other nations in order to share knowledge and allow all parties to take advantage of the best data available. Not only can the United States benefit from solutions developed in other countries, and vice versa, but the magnitude of impending global environmental problems may require the resources of more than one country.

DEPTH AND EFFECTIVENESS NEEDED

The federal environmental R&D effort covers a wide range of environmental problems, but the question before this Task Force is less one of breadth than it is one of efficiency and depth. Having been designed for a set of problems that no longer exists in its original form, our current federal environmental R&D effort is not structured in the most effective and comprehensive way to address either emerging problems or the increasingly complex interrelation of environmental issues that we face today. Change is needed, and in formulating our recommendations we have sought to pay particular attention to organizing federal R&D efforts so that they reflect an inclusive and forward-looking strategic philosophy, ensure effective monitoring and information management, contribute to a strong science and technology base, and enhance linkages within and outside the federal effort. Strong leadership from the President down will be the key to improving the environmental R&D effort.

PART II
RECOMMENDATIONS FOR STRENGTHENING
THE FEDERAL ENVIRONMENTAL R&D SYSTEM

3
INTRODUCTION

Our recommendations for strengthening federal environmental R&D programs fall into four categories: leadership and the research agenda, strengthening the R&D infrastructure, linking and coordinating programs, and building a strong intellectual base.

We first suggest several organizational and process modifications that we think would substantially improve the capacity of the Executive Office of the President and senior department and agency officials to direct federal R&D efforts. Effective leadership is essential in a highly decentralized research and development system. This is particularly true for environmental R&D programs, which require carefully orchestrated multidisciplinary and interagency programs.

Our second set of recommendations is directed at the individual departments and agencies that comprise our federal environmental R&D system. Every federal department and agency has a mission (although these missions often overlap and are sometimes not well defined), and each relies on R&D programs to varying degrees to support that mission. We present a series of recommendations designed to improve the effectiveness of several of the major federal R&D programs.

Our third set of recommendations points to a number of mechanisms to link federal programs to each other and to related programs in academia, nongovernmental organizations, and industry. We also underscore the importance of strong linkages between U.S. R&D programs and those of other nations. The national and global environmental problems facing the United States and the world are enormous and cannot be solved by one federal agency or even one nation. With this in mind, we suggest several ways to strengthen cooperative R&D efforts, both national and international.

Finally, we examine ways to ensure that the intellectual base of our environmental protection efforts is of adequate depth and breadth. Our educational system, from kindergarten to twelfth grade, to undergraduate, graduate, and postdoctoral training, must improve substantially if we are to meet the environmental challenges of the future. Although there are notable bright spots in our present educational system, there is much that can and must be improved in the years ahead.

As part of our examination of federal environmental R&D programs we considered a variety of organizational proposals, including suggestions to establish a National Institute for the Environment (NIE). We agree with several of the objectives of the NIE proposal: more support for environmental research, including ecological and interdisciplinary studies; improved storage of and access to data on environmental quality; and greater training opportunities for environmental scientists.[34] However, in working to find ways to achieve these and other objectives we have attempted, wherever possible, to build upon the existing federal infrastructure, improving and expanding established institutions. We recommend below that EPA establish and support up to six centers for environmental research. These centers would have some of the features of an NIE.

In the past twenty years a number of proposals to reorganize the federal government have been advanced. These have ranged from grouping all federal entities with environmental or natural resources responsibilities into a Department of Natural Resources, to elevating the Environmental Protection Agency to a cabinet-level department. The former would alter the organization of R&D programs substantially, while the latter would have less impact on them. In preparing our report we have assumed that a major federal reorganization is not likely and have consequently thought about changes in the R&D system in the context of the present general departmental and agency structures and the possible establishment of a Department of the Environment.

4
LEADERSHIP AND THE RESEARCH AGENDA

In guiding federal departments and agencies in their efforts to protect the environment, the President relies on several entities within the Executive Office to provide analysis and advice — most notably the Council on Environmental Quality (CEQ), the Office of Science and Technology Policy (OSTP), the Office of Management and Budget, and the Council of Economic Advisers. Our recommendations in this chapter focus on the critical roles of White House policymaking offices, and on the means to provide these organizations with the information and analysis they need to advise the President on environmental policy issues and to direct federal environmental programs toward national objectives.

■ **The White House apparatus for establishing environmental policy and for guiding federal environmental R&D programs should be strengthened by expanding the responsibilities of existing units in the Executive Office of the President and by establishing a new institutional capability to assess** scientific and technical information and to analyze environmental issues from the standpoint of economic, social, and political considerations.

THE OFFICE OF ENVIRONMENTAL QUALITY

■ *The mission of the existing White House Office of Environmental Quality (OEQ) should be expanded, giving it broad responsibility for developing environmental policies in the context of other considerations, particularly economic. The Office should also work to identify ways in which the activities of all federal departments and agencies can be directed toward sustainable development and risk-reduction objectives.*

The Council on Environmental Quality (CEQ) was established by the National Environmental Policy Act in 1969. Shortly afterward, the White House Office of Environmental Quality was established by the Environmental Quality Improvement Act of 1970.[35] CEQ has been the dominant organizational entity. However, over the past four years, CEQ has operated not as a council, but as an office administered by a chairman who also serves as the director of OEQ. We believe the activities of CEQ should be integrated into the Office of Environmental Quality. We considered other organizational mechanisms to provide a focal point for environmental policy-making in the White House, but building on the existing OEQ, rather than establishing an entirely new entity is, in our view, the most efficient approach.

A robust, analytically sophisticated, and influential Office of Environmental Quality is a critical component of the White House policy-making apparatus. Several fundamental changes are needed in the operations of the Office if it is to address the challenges of the 1990s and beyond. We believe that OEQ's mission should be administered by a director who functions simultaneously as the Assistant to the President for the Environment. In this capacity the director should lead efforts in the White House to develop environmental, sustainable development, and risk-related policy options, presenting proposals to the President and the Cabinet for their consideration. The director should be given broad authority to look across all departments and agencies and identify ways in which federal activities can be directed toward the environmental objectives of the President.

In developing policy proposals, the OEQ should work to integrate environmental, energy, and economic considerations. As discussed in an earlier Commission report, actions should be taken "to assure the stable and sustained functioning of a high-level mechanism concerned with linking environment, energy, and the economy."[36] We reaffirm the recommendations of that report: an expansion of staff expertise, particularly in the areas of science, engineering, energy, and economics, and a capability to develop integrated environment, energy, and economic policies.

OEQ should also work with OSTP to identify major R&D needs, to promote the improvement of risk assessment and risk management procedures, and to coordinate major R&D initiatives. In addition, OEQ should work closely with the Office of Management and Budget in guiding the budget process with respect to environmental programs.

INSTITUTE FOR ENVIRONMENTAL ASSESSMENT

■ *An Institute for Environmental Assessment (IEA) should be established to evaluate global and national environmental problems and to develop alternative approaches to them.*

Meeting the enormous environmental challenges of the future will require not only a major commitment to research and development, but the development of innovative environmental protection policies. The federal government currently lacks a critical mass of individuals who can assess the information resulting from our natural science research efforts and consider its implications in the context of current economic, social, and political realities. Although various federal agencies have offices devoted to policy planning and evaluation, these units are relatively small, and they appropriately devote their resources to issues pertinent to the missions of the agencies they support. With the exception of a small staff within the President's Council on Environmental Quality, there is no federal organization devoted to the comprehensive analysis of environmental policy.

We believe that the federal government's effectiveness in addressing environmental problems is severely limited by this lack of analytical and planning capability. Assessment is the bridge between science and policy.[37] Two major discontinuities now exist between the two: "One is that policymakers fail to understand the limits of what science can determine. And the second is that scientists very frequently fail to understand what the policy community really needs to know."[38] The federal government needs a mechanism to bridge the gap between science and policy.

We therefore recommend the establishment of an Institute for Environmental Assessment dedicated to the evaluation of global and national environmental problems, the achievement of sustainable development, the assessment of research and monitoring data, the evaluation of emerging environmental technologies, the development of economic, legal, and social analyses of mechanisms to address environmental problems, and the development and assessment of integrated strategies to address environmental problems. The IEA could convene environmental assessment committees to bring individuals from various federal departments and agencies together to evaluate specific environmental problems and ways to respond to them.[39] Consistent with the successful approach of the congressional Office of Technology Assessment, the IEA should consider optional strategies and policies to address environmental problems. It should not, however, *recommend* particular courses of action. These decisions are the responsibility of the Executive Office of the President, Congress, and the heads of federal departments and agencies.

The institute should be administered by a director who reports to the Director of the White House Office of Environmental Quality. We recommend that the IEA be provided with funds to undertake analyses within the institute itself and to support the work of individuals and institutions outside of the federal government through grants and contracts. At least half the institute's funding should be devoted to extramural studies conducted within nongovernmental organizations and academic institutions. Depending on its size and mission, an IEA could be located in the Executive Office, or in the Environmental Protection Agency or a proposed Department of the Environment. Alternatively, it could function as a quasigovernmental institution operated by a nongovernmental organization but reporting to the OEQ in the Executive Office, or to the Secretary of a Department of the Environment.

ENVIRONMENTAL RESEARCH AND MONITORING INITIATIVE

■ *The President, with the guidance and support of Congress, should undertake an Environmental Research and Monitoring Initiative, a long-term effort to bring all federal environmental R&D programs into a common policy framework.*

Through an Environmental Research and Monitoring Initiative the President can take the actions necessary to develop an integrated federal environmental R&D program, an essential step toward better directing federal scientific and engineering resources toward national and global problems. This initiative could be a component of a broader National Environmental Strategy, which we understand the National Commission on the Environment will recommend in its upcoming report.[40] The Initiative should be guided by the Director of the Office of Environmental Quality (discussed above) and the Director of the Office of Science and Technology Policy and should involve the key administrators of federal R&D programs, as well as the Office of Management and Budget. The group should work with the Office of Management and Budget to devise coherent short- and long-term R&D plans for each agency, including explicit goals and milestones.[41] These plans should include a description of the contributions of agencies and departments to broad federal program objectives, keeping in mind the R&D requirements of individual agencies and departments in pursuing their missions.

To be successful, an initiative of this scope will require the guidance and support of Congress. Congressional authorization, appropriations, and oversight responsibilities with respect to federal environmental programs are divided among numerous congressional committees and subcommittees in both the Senate and the House of Representatives. If federal environmental R&D programs are to be properly coordinated and directed at well-defined goals, Congress, like the President, must provide clear and decisive leadership. The Carnegie Commission's Committee on Congress will soon be issuing a report on the challenges Congress faces in addressing science and technology issues of this kind.

A high-level initiative of this kind would give environmental R&D a higher priority in federal activities, would provide leadership to this critical area of science and technology policy, and would coordinate the diverse activities of federal departments and agencies. In the recommendations below, we suggest mechanisms to achieve these ends.

OFFICE OF SCIENCE AND TECHNOLOGY POLICY

■ *The Office of Science and Technology Policy (OSTP) should coordinate a broader array of environmental R&D activities.*

The Office of Science and Technology Policy within the Executive Office of the President is home to the Federal Coordinating Council on Science, Engineering, and Technology (FCCSET), which has proven to be an effective mechanism for coordinating the management of certain federal R&D programs. The U.S. Global Change Research Program, for example, is administered under FCCSET through its Committee on Earth Sciences. In fiscal year 1992, the $1.3 billion program coordinated federal R&D activities in eleven departments and agencies and served as the focal point for interactions with the international scientific community, agencies of other governments, and the private sector.[42]

We recommend that OSTP use FCCSET to aid in the development of coherent federal environmental R&D programs to address problems that cut across departments and agencies. Close interaction between OSTP, as it coordinates R&D programs, the Office of Environmental Quality, as it develops environmental policy and research needs, and the Office of Management and Budget, as it devises budget priorities, is essential if the federal government is to achieve an integrated and forward-looking environmental protection program.

5
STRENGTHENING THE FEDERAL R&D INFRASTRUCTURE

Our federal environmental R&D system is broad, diverse, and highly decentralized. Led by the intramural programs of the Environmental Protection Agency and the U.S. Geological Survey, and complemented by the extensive extramural programs of the National Institute of Environmental Health Sciences and the National Science Foundation, the principal federal environmental R&D infrastructure is comprised of programs in numerous departments and agencies, each with a different mission and a different set of strengths and weaknesses. The recommendations below are aimed at strengthening the individual and collective R&D efforts of these organizations, as well as their ability to contribute to the evaluation and implementation of environmental policies.

■ **The federal environmental R&D infrastructure should be strengthened by improving and streamlining EPA's existing laboratory organization, by supporting a group of nonfederal Environmental Research**

Institutes, by organizing a new U.S. Environmental Monitoring Agency and a National Center for Environmental Information, and by enhancing R&D capabilities in several key federal agencies.

ENVIRONMENTAL PROTECTION AGENCY

NEW NATIONAL LABORATORIES

■ *The Environmental Protection Agency's existing laboratory structure, now comprised of 12 laboratories, should be consolidated to create a National Ecological Systems Laboratory, a National Environmental Monitoring Systems Laboratory, a National Environmental Engineering Laboratory, and a National Health Effects Research Laboratory.*

The efforts of EPA's Office of Research and Development (ORD) are critical to achieving the nation's environmental protection objectives. Since its inception, EPA has struggled with the optimal organization of the research units within the ORD and the agency as a whole. Several years ago William D. Ruckelshaus, EPA's first administrator, described the challenges the agency faced when it was first organized in 1970:

> Our efforts to establish the scientific base presupposed by the environmental laws were hindered by the difficulties of managing the six different scientific establishments that EPA had inherited. Our scientific resources were housed in 56 separate laboratories scattered across the country. From the first, it was extremely difficult to convey to EPA's scientific cadre the urgency of our need for authoritative findings to support the regulations we were obligated to turn out to the beat of those timetables in the legislation.[43]

If a Department of the Environment is established, the conflict between the need for information to support regulatory needs and the necessity to support long-term basic and applied research will remain. It will be critically important to achieve the proper balance between the two. Our recommendations below were developed with this concern in mind.

In recognition of the need to improve the scientific basis of its regulatory decisions, EPA has recently taken a number of steps to enhance the quality of its R&D programs. In responding to a recent report by an expert advisory panel, EPA is working to develop a more coherent science agenda, expand the use of science advisors within the agency, attract and retain outstanding scientists and engineers, and improve its interactions with other agencies and with academic and industrial research organizations.[44] These are important initiatives, and we applaud and support them. However, we believe that organizational innovations are also needed to advance EPA's R&D efforts. In addition, funding for ORD remains a chronic problem.

In 1984, the leaders of ten major environmental organizations and the CEOs of five major chemical companies wrote to Congressman Edward P. Boland, Chairman of the House Appropriations Subcommittee on VA, HUD, and Independent Agencies and strongly urged him to increase the fiscal year 1985 budget to EPA's Office of Research and Development by $101 million more than the Administration's request. The group spoke of their "deep concern that the scientific base on which the agency's regulatory decisions are founded has been seriously eroded in recent years by severe cuts in the research and development budget of the EPA."[45] They pointed out that as measured in constant dollars, the ORD budget for FY 1985 was 15 percent less than in 1973 when ORD was created, even though Congress had passed several laws requiring additional R&D support during that period.

Today, severe funding constraints continue to limit ORD's effectiveness.[46] Despite substantial increases in R&D responsibilities ORD's budget, in constant dollars, has increased only modestly over the last decade, and because of severe limitations on full-time equivalents, a disproportionate share of the workforce at ORD laboratories is on-site contractors.[47] Although our report focuses on organizational issues, it is clear that organizational changes alone will not lead to improvements in the scientific capacity of EPA. Substantial funding increases will be required as well.

A National Ecological Systems Laboratory

An EPA National Ecological Systems Laboratory (NESL) should be formed by combining the six existing EPA R&D laboratories. A new headquarters site would be established for the national laboratory, with some of the existing laboratories continuing to operate as field sites under the direction of the national laboratory (see Figures 4 and 5, pages 66 and 67). The existing laboratories are located at Corvallis, Oregon; Duluth, Minnesota; Gulf Breeze, Florida; Narragansett, Rhode Island; Ada, Oklahoma; and Athens, Georgia.

This organizational arrangement would offer numerous advantages. First, it would create a critical mass of researchers and resources focused on understanding how environmental insults propagate through ecosystems. Research programs would be cross-media (air, water, terrestrial) and multidisciplinary in orientation.

Through the creation of such a national resource, EPA's Office of Research and Development should be able to attract a nationally prominent scientist–administrator to direct the laboratory. The director should report to the Assistant Administrator for Research and Development (or the Assistant Secretary for Research and Development in the proposed cabinet-level Department of Environment).

By creating this laboratory and attracting a prominent director, EPA would bring into existence a powerful counterbalance to the constant pressure from the regulatory offices for continuous emergency response support. Given the critical needs of the regulatory offices in dealing with science- and technology-driven problems, it does not make sense to separate such a national laboratory from EPA or a Department of the Environment. It is necessary, however, to moderate the surges in demand for support from the regulatory offices.

Because of its critical mass and its perceived greater importance, a national laboratory should be better positioned to compete for limited resources. At this time, each of the six small R&D laboratories must compete individually for its funds and staff. Justification for increased support is difficult, given each laboratory's limited mission.

Finally, because of its improved stature, such a national laboratory would operate on a more equal footing with other major federal laboratories and leading scientific organizations.

The major disadvantage of combining the six EPA laboratories into a national ecological laboratory is the geographical distribution of the existing laboratories. This decentralization makes overall program management difficult, and it will take some time for the several parts of a new national laboratory to begin working in an integrated fashion. It will also require leadership to develop a vision of a truly national laboratory.

This problem goes to the heart of the nation's environmental dilemma — how to manage our national environmental resources while respecting the biodiversity encompassed in the nation. We think that it is more important to fashion an integrated ecological research program under a single administrative entity than it is to attempt to coordinate a highly decentralized system.

Some may argue that this experiment has already been conducted, and that the attempt failed. In 1973, EPA's Office of Research and Development reorganized all of its laboratories into three National Environmental Research Centers (NERCs). One NERC, placed under the direction of the Corvallis laboratory, encompassed most of the ecological effects and processes laboratories identified above. Communications and coordination among the laboratories and between the NERC headquarters and the Washington-based ORD headquarters were judged to be ineffective. In 1975, the NERCs were abolished, and the ORD laboratory structure returned to its present configuration.

In our opinion, the NERC experiment failed for several reasons. First, too much was attempted at one time, and the entire ORD organization was thrown into turmoil by the change. Second, the affected laboratories, which had previously operated quite autonomously under the Federal Water Pollution Control Administration, had not been prepared to function as

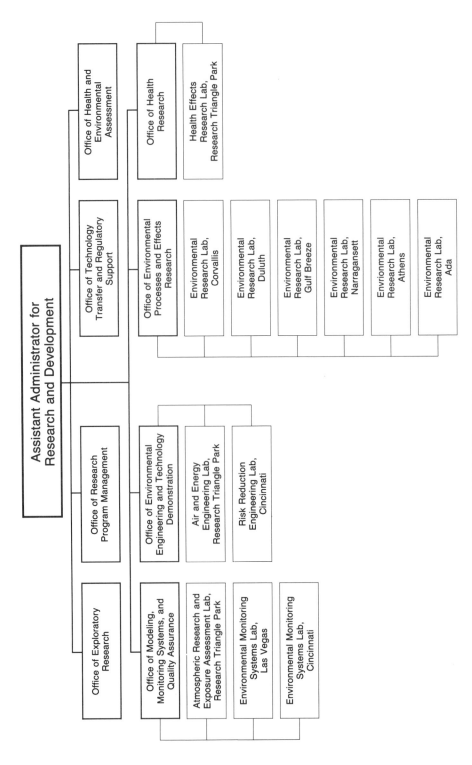

Figure 4. Current EPA Office of Research and Development Organization

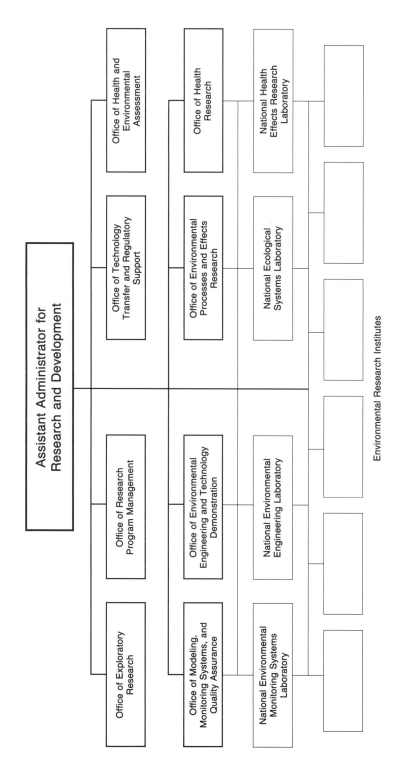

Figure 5. Recommended Future EPA Office of Research and Development Organization

a team. Third, appointing one of the "peer" laboratory directors as NERC director exacerbated the competitive tendencies in the laboratories. The proposal outlined above is designed to avoid these shortcomings, while trying to achieve an integrated program.

A National Environmental Monitoring Systems Laboratory

We propose that three laboratories in EPA's Office of Research and Development devoted to environmental monitoring be combined to form a National Environmental Monitoring Systems Laboratory (NEMSL). The three existing laboratories whose operations would be integrated are the Environmental Monitoring System Laboratories in Cincinnati, Ohio, and Las Vegas, Nevada, and the Atmospheric Research and Exposure Assessment Laboratory in Research Triangle Park, North Carolina. A headquarters site should be established for the NEMSL, with the existing laboratories continuing to operate as field sites under its direction.

The NEMSL would likely enjoy important synergies in monitoring technologies, analytical techniques, and statistical analysis, resulting in cost reductions, especially in cross-media monitoring efforts. The laboratory would also create a critical mass of researchers and resources focused on the technical foundations of environmental monitoring.

A significant challenge in combining the three EPA laboratories is overcoming the cultural differences among the three groups of scientists and engineers. Although the underlying chemistry is essentially the same, the groups evolved under separate air, water, and radiological pollution agencies. These differences can be overcome in time, with many synergies developing as operations are integrated. If a U.S. Environmental Monitoring Agency is established, as recommended later in this report, some or all of the activities of the NEMSL should be integrated with those of, or transferred to, the new agency.

A National Environmental Engineering Laboratory

We recommend that a single National Environmental Engineering Laboratory (NEEL) be established by combining the existing EPA Risk Reduction Engineering Laboratory in Cincinnati, Ohio, and the Air and Energy Engineering Laboratory in Research Triangle Park, North Carolina. The main laboratory, in North Carolina, would focus on air and energy engineering, and the Cincinnati component of the laboratory would focus on water-quality–related laboratory research and risk reduction. The NEEL should work to advance the development of innovative environmental technologies and should forge relationships with industry in advancing toward common goals. The laboratory should work in conjunction with other federal departments and agencies to promote the development and diffusion of environmental technologies through a federal interagency Environmental Technologies Program discussed later in this report (see page 78).

A National Health Effects Research Laboratory

We recommend raising the EPA Health Effects Research Laboratory in Research Triangle Park, North Carolina, to the same status as the other three proposed EPA national laboratories. This would involve no significant change in the mission or staffing of this laboratory. The National Health Effects Research Laboratory should work closely with the National Institute of Environmental Health Sciences in planning and implementing research efforts.

Leadership and Cooperation

Each of the four proposed EPA national laboratories should be directed by an outstanding scientist or engineer of national stature who has the administrative skills necessary to direct programs of this scope. Every effort should be made to attract outstanding scientists, engineers, and other personnel to these organizations. Federal personnel should interact with individuals in the proposed Environmental Research Institutes (discussed in the next section) and in academia, nongovernmental organizations, and industry. In addition, it is essential that all four laboratories work closely with the proposed Institute for Environmental Assessment (see page 59) in evaluating environmental problems and alternative approaches to addressing them.

ENVIRONMENTAL RESEARCH INSTITUTES

■ *EPA should establish and support up to six major Environmental Research Institutes (ERIs) associated with academic institutions and nongovernmental organizations across the country.*

Today, the U.S. Environmental Protection Agency provides support to a set of four university-based Environmental Research Centers, or "centers of excellence." Each center specializes in a particular research topic of interest to the agency, receiving about $1 million per year from EPA. The work of the centers is severely limited by inadequate funding. Furthermore, they are typically organized as a component of a university or college, which presents both advantages and disadvantages.

EPA's Centers of Excellence program was initiated during the Carter administration, when zero-based budgeting was used to prepare EPA's budget submission to OMB. While there was some support for longer-term R&D in the regulatory offices, there was also intense competition for resources (both dollars and personnel) to meet the legislative requirements of the Toxic Substances Control Act and other laws and regulations. In addition, in the late 1970s no one in EPA was advocating larger centers. The regulatory offices viewed the use of funds for such centers as a diversion from the agency's mission, and R&D staff generally felt the centers program was diverting money away from the laboratories. The result was that the new centers initiative was approved but its budget was limited (about $3 million in 1979). This funding was then used to establish multiple centers. Until recently, EPA supported eight centers at a funding level of approximately $500,000 each.

In order for an environmental center of excellence to have significant impact, it must have adequate resources. Annual funding of $500,000 is woefully inadequate to support the high-quality research teams needed to attack what are complex problems requiring multidisciplinary investigations. Subcritical funding results in the all too typical university center model—a few part-time faculty researchers, a few postdoctoral researchers, and a few graduate students. There are generally no full-time researchers and technicians, and equipment and instrumentation are shared, not dedicated.

To ensure its effectiveness in addressing the major environmental challenges facing the nation and the world, funding for each ERI should gradually rise to the level of $10 to $15 million annually for at least five years. In areas that require extensive support equipment, such as a research ship or sophisticated analytical instruments, additional funding should be provided. A full-time director, with world class credentials, and full-time researchers and technicians should make up the core of the institute, with faculty, postdoctoral students, and graduate students supplementing the full-time core staff.

ERIs should operate as EPA's principal extramural research units and should be complemented by a strong, well-funded extramural grants program. The ERIs should cooperate with the four EPA National Laboratories described above. The ERIs should focus on problem-oriented themes that require multidisciplinary research efforts that cut across the missions of the intramural National Laboratories. The institutes would thus function as more flexible, problem-oriented, multidisciplinary components of a Department of the Environment, thereby complementing the structured, discipline-oriented intramural National Laboratories. We envision a two-way flow of personnel between the National Laboratories and the ERIs. This would give government scientists, engineers, and social scientists an opportunity to benefit from the career growth and educational opportunities offered in the university and nongovernmental setting. It would also enhance the National Laboratories by bringing some of the best scientists and engineers in the nation into government laboratories for extended periods.

After considering the views of a full range of experts within and outside the federal government, the EPA Science Advisory Board (SAB) should make recommendations to the EPA Administrator regarding the missions of the Institutes. The SAB should examine other similar research organizations operating through the National Institutes of Health and the Department of Energy and should make recommendations to EPA's Office of Research and Development as to how the best features of these organizations can be incorporated into EPA's institutes. The ERIs should then be awarded through a merit-based competition.

The ERIs' charter and organization are critical to their success. Institutes of the size envisioned here cannot function as academic subunits. While it is important for the institutes to have a close affiliation with a university (or with several universities), it is essential that they not operate as a component of a university, especially not as a component of a single college or department. The institutes could report to the research vice presidents or to the presidents of universities, or affiliated but autonomous not-for-profit institutes could be established outside, but nearby, the universities.

A number of organizations have demonstrated that they can effectively operate research institutes staffed with full-time employees under research administrations separate from academic administrations. Faculty and students move back and forth from the academic side to the research institute once the rules and expectations are negotiated and understood. The success of this approach seems to be highly correlated with the culture of the individual university.

A more recent trend is the establishment of affiliated not-for-profit centers. Many of these organizations have been created in the last decade as states have expanded their support of technology-driven economic development. One distinct advantage of such centers is that proprietary work with industry is greatly facilitated in the autonomous centers. Faculty and students can still do nonproprietary work within these organizations, but they would recognize that if they choose to work on proprietary projects, publication of their work may be delayed or precluded. If an ERI's mission requires close cooperation with industry, then the not-for-profit approach can operate in a typical business fashion, rather than following university calendars and administrative procedures.

ENVIRONMENTAL MONITORING AGENCY

▪ *A new federal agency, the U.S. Environmental Monitoring Agency (EMA), should be organized by combining the National Oceanic and Atmospheric Administration, now within the Department of Commerce, with the U.S. Geological Survey, now within the Department of the Interior.*

Monitoring, mapping, inventorying, and forecasting with respect to the national and global environment are the cornerstones of federal environmental protection efforts. Documenting the characteristics of our air, land, and water resources is an enormous task that is now primarily undertaken by the U.S. Geological Survey (USGS), the National Oceanic and Atmospheric Administration (NOAA), and to a lesser extent the National Aeronautics and Space Administration (NASA) and the Environmental Protection Agency (EPA). The present and future missions of NOAA and USGS are more similar to each other than they are to the missions of the departments in which they reside. Consequently, we believe that these organizations should merge to form the U.S. Environmental Monitoring Agency (EMA).[48]

The EMA should make use of data developed by NASA, EPA, the Fish and Wildlife Service, the National Institute for Environmental Health Sciences, and other agencies. It should maintain close ties with the National Aeronautics and Space Administration in an effort to link the Earth Observing System (EOS) and related environmental monitoring activities with its programs. Certain EPA activities, such as the Environmental Monitoring and Assessment Program (EMAP),[49] should be transferred into the EMA. The Agency's mission should include monitoring and evaluation of both natural processes and the social activities that are driving forces for environmental deterioration. These include consumption patterns, population growth, and use of modes of transportation. It should include biological surveys as well as geological surveys, mapping, and inventorying of both the biological and physical environment.

We believe that EMA should operate as an independent federal agency or as an entity within a Department of the Environment. Independence is important for an agency whose mission is devoted to monitoring the state of the environment and the progress of the nation in achieving environmental protection objectives. If a Department of the Environment is established at some point in the future, EMA could become a component of this organization; however, the agency should operate independently of the regulatory programs of a department. The EMA should maintain ties with the Institute for Environmental Assessment, providing the Institute with data to support its evaluation of national and global problems.

THE U.S. GEOLOGICAL SURVEY

The USGS has operated quite autonomously within the Department of the Interior. Over the years it has developed a reputation for excellence in its monitoring and research activities. USGS is responsible for gathering information and conducting analyses of land resources, minerals and energy resources, and geologic hazards. It is also responsible for studies in surface water and groundwater assessment and protection, toxic and nuclear substances hydrology, acid rain, and climate change hydrology. USGS is a key player in the federal government's Global Change Research Program, contributing to the effort to understand natural earth processes and the impacts of human activities on earth systems. It is also a leader in the development of information systems using advanced computer technologies. For example, it recently produced a prototype interactive CD-ROM science journal on the Arctic that has been widely acclaimed as a research and communications tool.[50] About $367 million was spent on environmental R&D in the USGS in 1992.

All of this work would continue in EMA. The 1879 charter of USGS sets forth its mission as the "classification of the public lands and examination of the geological structure, mineral resources, and products of the national domain."[51] Today, more than 90 percent of the USGS program budget is devoted to monitoring activities in its National Mapping Program, Geologic Investigations, and Water Resources Investigations Divisions.

THE NATIONAL OCEANIC AND ATMOSPHERIC ADMINISTRATION

NOAA was established by President Nixon in 1970 at approximately the same time, and in the same manner, as the Environmental Protection Agency.[52] The creation of NOAA had been recommended by the Stratton Commission, an independent panel of scientific experts assembled by Congress in the late 1960s to review the present and future needs of marine affairs, including oceanography, marine resources, ocean engineering, and education. Although the Commission had advised that it be an independent agency, two of the larger existing organizations that were brought together to form NOAA were located in the Department of Commerce, and it was ultimately placed there.

NOAA's Mission

NOAA's general mission is to monitor the global environment, predict environmental changes, and provide the public with environmental informa-

---

Box 4.   Monitoring the Ocean Environment*

Long-term monitoring of the environment is nowhere more important than in the ocean. With its large heat capacity and its mobility, the ocean plays a key role in the climate system. Although our knowledge of the ocean and its processes is limited because of the vast range of time and space scales involved, we do know that the ocean acts regionally as a buffer and affects the coastal climate. Globally, the ocean acts as a heat source that forces atmospheric convection and wind and drives weather patterns.

With new technical and computer modeling techniques, a number of major international research programs are being carried out to develop an adequate understanding of the ocean and its interaction with the atmosphere and continental margins. One example of success in this research is that scientists are now producing forecasts of the climate anomalies due to El Niño. But information on long-term changes is lacking. Consequently, the ability of scientists to model and predict changes in the ocean on a broader scale is limited. One proposal to facilitate advances in this area is a Global Ocean Observing System (GOOS), the oceans component of the internationally planned Global Climate Observing System. With adequate support and institutional infrastructure, it is possible that by the end of this decade investigators will be able to maintain an ocean model that could be used for forecasts of ocean eddies, El Niño, and dispersion of pollutants, and for other practical purposes.

It is important to begin as soon as possible to put in place the systems that can provide global information; such systems include satellite-based instruments, automatic fixed and floating buoys that transmit information to shore, acoustic monitoring systems, and the necessary data links.

Institutional support is the key to the success of GOOS. At present NOAA is the lead agency, with strong contributions from the NSF, which has been the key supporter of global research programs. The DoD, DoE, and USGS also provide support for significant elements of global observing systems. A new U.S. Environmental Monitoring Agency would provide a strong institutional home for a program such as the GOOS.

---

* D. James Baker contributed to this box.

---

tion and forecasting. It is charged with monitoring and data collection and analysis for the oceans and atmosphere, including weather forecasting and coastal and ocean research (see Box 4). Two pieces of NOAA scientific research—a time series of increasing atmospheric carbon dioxide levels over the past three decades, and modeling of greenhouse gases and their role in global warming—have been praised by both scientists and policymakers.

Because of its technical expertise, it has become one of the premier agencies involved in the Global Change Research Program and has shaped much of the current debate and information about global climate change. NOAA also has taken the lead in researching the environmental effects of the Persian Gulf War oil spills on the western shore of the Persian Gulf,[53] and it has sponsored research indicating that CFC substitutes may cause more damage to the stratosphere than originally postulated.[54]

Although NOAA has contributed significantly to atmospheric and oceanic science, its separation from other basic research environmental R&D agencies and its location within the Department of Commerce have resulted in less visibility than that of other environmental agencies. Furthermore, its current position has made it vulnerable to budget cuts.

Weaknesses and Isolation

Today, NOAA suffers from several weaknesses that are directly related to its location within Commerce and its consequent isolation. First, NOAA's mission includes a combination of research and environmental services. In recent years, its mission has evolved away from basic research to emphasize "environmental services" in business and economics.[55] This shift in philosophy impedes NOAA's ability to plan and carry out environmental R&D. Commerce is a business-oriented department created to help American industry become more competitive, to promote trade and export in American goods and services, and to speed up commercialization of new technologies. As a science agency, NOAA's location within the Department of Commerce makes little sense.[56] Although NOAA accounts for more than half the Department's budget, it does not command half the Secretary of Commerce's attention.

Second, NOAA's funding has fluctuated greatly over the past decade. During the 1980s, for example, the Reagan administration proposed 10 percent cuts in NOAA's funding each year. Congress resisted these cuts, and NOAA's budget remained more or less constant throughout the decade. However, because of inflation, its budget in real dollars actually declined.[57] Although the recent Global Change Research Program has resulted in a reversal of that trend, the lack of adequate funding during the 1980s caused NOAA to defer many capital improvements that were needed to maintain the technical infrastructure that supports its environmental R&D efforts.[58]

Third, NOAA has failed to establish strong ties to universities and to the private sector.[59] Universities and private businesses could greatly assist the agency in carrying out its environmental research agenda and in building a strong constituency for the agency.

ELIMINATING WEAKNESSES, CAPITALIZING ON STRENGTHS

The creation of an independent Environmental Monitoring Agency would capitalize on the strengths of both USGS and NOAA. Inefficiencies in overlapping or duplicated capital investment and monitoring activities could be eliminated. Existing weaknesses resulting from their organizational locations, particularly NOAA's, could be overcome. And, perhaps more important, monitoring and analysis of all the earth's resources—oceans, atmosphere, and terrestrial—would be brought together under one agency, which could approach them with a comprehensive, unified perspective. We believe that the EMA should operate initially as an independent federal agency; however, if a Department of the Environment is established, it would be advantageous to make the EMA a component of the Department.[60] The proposed federal environmental R&D infrastructure incorporating the changes we have recommended is shown in Figure 6.

NATIONAL CENTER FOR ENVIRONMENTAL INFORMATION

■ *A National Center for Environmental Information (NCEI) should be established within the proposed U.S. Environmental Monitoring Agency.*

A National Center for Environmental Information should serve as a focal point for the storage and retrieval of information generated from a range of sources, primarily federal departments and agencies, but also state and local governments, academia, industry, and nongovernmental organizations. The center should be responsible for developing policies to ensure that environmental data are properly stored and are readily accessible to all users.

The center should not be responsible for monitoring activities—it should work, however, to ensure that the data developed by federal investigators and those in the private sector are stored in compatible formats, and that they are properly catalogued. In most cases, individual federal programs, agencies, and departments would continue to maintain their own databases. In this sense the center would function primarily as an electronic access point and would not duplicate or supersede existing data storage capabilities. For example, the center would not duplicate the extensive toxicological information available at the National Library of Medicine, but would inform potential users of the information that is available and explain how to access it.

Efforts to coordinate the development, use, sharing, and dissemination of geographic data are already under way through the Federal Geo-

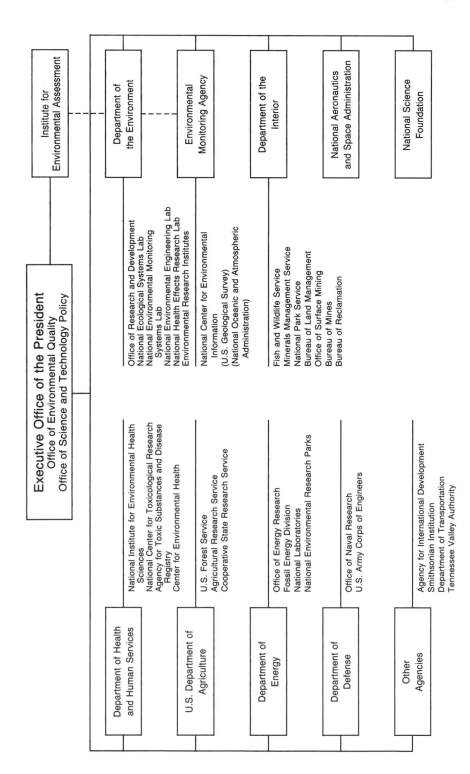

Figure 6. Proposed Federal Environmental R&D Infrastructure

graphic Data Committee. Coordination activities of this kind will become increasingly important as massive quantities of data on the state of the environment are generated in the years ahead.

One important activity of the National Center and the Environmental Monitoring Agency should be the development of national biological inventories, a concerted effort to document the nation's plant and animal resources.[61] Such information is critical in documenting the impact of pollutants and other forms of disruption on ecosystems, in evaluating biological diversity, and in monitoring the progress of environmental protection efforts.

ENVIRONMENTAL TECHNOLOGIES PROGRAM

■ *A federal interagency Environmental Technologies Program should be established to promote and support the development of advanced technologies by federal agencies, universities, industry, and nongovernmental organizations.*

Responding to the environmental challenges of the decade ahead will require the development of a full range of advanced technologies to minimize waste, enhance energy efficiency, promote agricultural productivity, and limit the release of pollutants into the environment. These include biotechnologies that can limit the use of traditional toxic pesticides, minimize the application of fertilizers, and enhance the productivity of crops. Programs supporting the development of environmental technologies are under way throughout the federal government.[62] Federal agencies, particularly EPA, must modify their regulatory procedures to encourage these kinds of technological innovation,[63] but regulatory incentives alone are not sufficient.

We recommend the establishment of a federal interagency Environmental Technologies Program that would provide support to federal agencies and the private sector through grants, loans, and cooperative agreements to promote the development and diffusion of these technologies. EPA, or a Department of the Environment, should function as the lead federal agency, providing funds to other agencies, industries, academic institutions, and nongovernmental institutions as appropriate to support new and existing technology development programs. Government support should primarily be for precompetitive, general technologies[64] or activities leading to useful nonproprietary knowledge — knowledge that is broadly applicable, but whose potential applications can be predicted, with some degree of accuracy, in advance.[65]

EPA has experience in administering programs of this kind. In the middle to late 1970s, the Federal Interagency Energy/Environment R&D Program successfully coordinated federal R&D efforts, with EPA providing funds to other federal agencies through interagency agreements. A similar program focused on technology development would help ensure an integrated federal approach to technology development. Congressman Joseph P. Kennedy has introduced legislation to establish a program of this kind.[66]

NATIONAL AERONAUTICS AND SPACE ADMINISTRATION

■ *The National Aeronautics and Space Administration should closely link its environmental monitoring activities with those of other federal departments and agencies and of other nations.*

Satellite-based earth observing systems make a fundamental contribution to understanding, describing, and monitoring the biosphere. Such satellites can support research efforts dealing with problems of climate change and ozone depletion, operational systems such as weather forecasting, and commercial interests in forestry, agriculture, mineral resources, and land use planning. But despite broad international interest and widespread activities, space-based remote sensing has followed an erratic course. In part, the imperfections of this approach have been due to the high cost of long-term remote sensing from space. Given the wide interest in remote sensing, it is essential to make future earth-observing systems as efficient as possible. Over the long term, it seems most efficient to procure a standard satellite and operating system worldwide. This would involve merging and coordinating governmental and commercial interests with new and innovative intergovernmental and private arrangements (see Box 5).

Over the years, various alternatives to an intergovernmental coordinating mechanism have been suggested as part of the efforts to reduce the cost of existing and future government and commercial observing systems. One possibility would be to construct an international network of earth-observing systems, analogous to the successful INTELSAT and INMARSAT of the telecommunications world, with all countries benefiting from improved, more reliable, and less costly services.

A wide range of institutions use remote sensing, including international, national, and state agencies; commercial firms; academic institutions; and individuals. These users receive data from two sources: satellite systems funded and operated by governments and private-sector operations. The market for land data alone has proven insufficient to sustain a remote sensing program. In many cases, commercial firms prefer to use aircraft-based remote sensing to meet their specialized needs, rather than rely on

Box 5. International Approaches to Space-Based
Remote Sensing

Difficulties with remote sensing arrangements abound. A large gap in the satellite monitoring of stratospheric ozone depletion is likely to open in 1995, when the U.S.-led Upper Air Research Satellite (UARS) stops functioning. This leaves a three-year gap until the earliest possible launch of a similar satellite as part of the U.S.-led Earth Observing System (EOS). But the latest plan for EOS from the U.S. National Aeronautics and Space Administration would further delay the first launch of instruments to monitor changes in stratospheric ozone. NASA is preparing plans that call for the launch of EOS atmospheric chemistry experiments in 2000 or 2002, rather than, as originally planned, in 1998. During this period, other satellites will carry total ozone mapping spectrometers, which measure the total amount of ozone in the column of atmosphere beneath a satellite. But it is also important to record in detail the chemical changes occurring in the stratosphere.

The situation with respect to climate monitoring is in many ways worse, largely due to the complexity of the systems that must be monitored. Again, EOS will provide valuable data, but there will be gaps in the monitoring of important parameters. Problems have also plagued the gathering and dissemination of surface data, which is of substantial commercial interest. The U.S. Landsat program includes as one of the principal requirements in granting licenses to operators a provision that data be made available on a public nondiscriminatory basis.

Fifteen nations have built ground stations to receive and process Landsat data, which is transmitted by a radio link from a polar-orbiting spacecraft. These stations cost about $20 million to build, and about $3 million each year to operate. Two spacecraft now in orbit are coming to the end of their service life. A sixth replacement spacecraft has been much delayed, and it is inevitable that there will be an interruption in service for several years. As a consequence, users around the world are modifying their ground stations to operate with the French Spot system, which provides similar information.

In 1987, the Soviet Union began to offer high-resolution photographs obtained from its KFA-1000 and other satellites to customers outside the Soviet bloc at a competitive price. The European Space Agency also intends to provide Landsat-type data. A number of other countries, including Japan, India, Indonesia, and Brazil, are developing or have recently launched remote sensing satellites.

In view of the gaps in data coverage and overlaps in land sensing data, several suggestions have been put forward to attempt to correct the situation. Prime Minister John Major of the United Kingdom has suggested that the problem could be addressed by the Committee on Earth Observing Satellites (CEOS), comprised of members of most of the countries with an interest in remote sensing satellites. The committee's objectives are to optimize the benefits of space-borne earth observation through cooperation of its members in mission planning and to develop compatible data products, formats, services, applications, and policies.

satellite information that is available to all. It appears, however, that governments themselves could constitute a market, based on their own needs for land, meteorological, and oceanographic remote sensing services. Other users would add to this market. With a large enough market, viable private-sector operations could be established to provide data to all users.

NASA's Earth Observing System (EOS) is designed to evolve over a 15-year period into a comprehensive system to collect and distribute remote sensing data on the atmosphere, oceans, and land surfaces. The cornerstone of the EOS effort is a group of space-based observatories that is now scheduled to begin collecting data shortly after the turn of the century. The data will be processed, stored, and distributed to researchers through the EOS Data and Information Systems (EOSDIS). EOSDIS will be an extraordinarily large data system, and, given its importance in monitoring the global environment, it is critically important that it be carefully designed and that it take advantage of new and emerging advanced technologies.[67] We believe that EOSDIS should be linked closely with the monitoring data systems of the proposed Environmental Monitoring Agency.

NATIONAL INSTITUTE OF ENVIRONMENTAL HEALTH SCIENCES

■ *The new research and training programs at the National Institute of Environmental Health Sciences should be expanded, and the Institute should establish closer ties with EPA's health research program.*

The National Institute of Environmental Health Sciences (NIEHS) bridges the basic research typical of NIH and academic biology and the more applied toxicological and epidemiological research needed for hazard identification and risk assessment. NIEHS recently undertook an internal reorganization to encourage multidisciplinary integrated research efforts.[68]

We believe that the Institute's research programs, both intramural and extramural, should expand steadily over the next decade. In particular, we recommend that NIEHS-sponsored training programs, now about $10 million, be doubled over the next four years to provide adequate numbers of well-trained environmental health scientists to industry, academia, and to the government research and regulatory agencies.

In 1988, the Public Health Service released an extensive study of the environmental health work force that presented a series of recommendations to help ensure that future personnel needs can be met.[69] Furthermore, research programs at NIEHS and EPA are directed at many common goals. We suggest that NIEHS and EPA's Office of Research and Development, particularly the Health Effects Research Laboratory (or the proposed

National Health Effects Research Laboratory) forge new cooperative research agreements. Both the Health Effects Laboratory and NIEHS are located in Research Triangle Park, North Carolina, which should make it easier to build on NIEHS's basic research strengths and EPA's applied research capabilities.

DEPARTMENT OF THE INTERIOR

■ *The Department of the Interior should develop a long-range plan for its environmental R&D activities and should work to integrate and focus its programs in the context of clearly defined goals.*

   The Department of the Interior is the caretaker of the nation's public lands and waterways. It is a large department in which environmental research and development play a relatively small role. Thus, while it carries out environmental research in all five of its divisions, its programs are decentralized and are not coordinated across the agency. The department's environmental R&D programs lack planning and coherence. Its research programs are underfunded and reactive, and little effort is directed to coordinating research across programs within the department. A long-range plan for environmental R&D would help direct department resources towards well-defined objectives.

NATIONAL PARK SERVICE

■ *The National Park Service should establish a strong environmental research and monitoring program to build the knowledge base necessary to protect the resources of the National Park system.*

   Over the past 30 years the Park Service has been advised on several occasions of the value of establishing a substantive environmental research program. In 1963, the NRC noted that "Research by the National Park Service has lacked continuity, coordination, and depth . . . has been marked by expediency rather than long-term considerations . . . has lacked direction . . . has been fragmented."[70] In the years that followed little significant improvement in research programs resulted, and in 1977 the National Research Council concluded that

> the National Park Service has reached a time in its history, and in the history of the nation, when science and research should be given a much greater and clearly recognized responsibility in policymaking, planning, and operations.

> Seat-of-the-pants guesses in resource preservation and management are open to challenge and do not stand up well in court or in the forum of public opinion.[71]

This year, an NRC report pointed out that, after almost a dozen reports over the past 30 years by various groups, little progress has been made in establishing a credible research program within the Park Service. The latest report calls for an explicit legislative mandate for a research mission in the National Park Service, including separate funding and reporting autonomy for the science program. The program should include a chief scientist and an external science advisory board.[72]

We support the NRC's recommendations for building a substantial research program within the National Park Service. The little progress made over the past 30 years in building a credible research unit makes it clear that establishing such a program will require stronger backing from Congress, the President, and the Secretary of the Interior.

BUREAU OF LAND MANAGEMENT

■ *The Bureau of Land Management should expand its environmental monitoring and technology programs and seek the assistance of other federal agencies in devising land use, biological resources management, waste management, and monitoring programs to protect public lands and to ensure their productive use in the future.*

The Bureau of Land Management (BLM) is responsible for managing 272 million acres of public lands. The Federal Land Policy and Management Act of 1976 requires that these multiple use lands be managed in the long-term public interest without impairing productivity or environmental quality.[73] However, these lands have not been properly maintained, and the biological resources have not been protected. Improper use and carelessness has resulted in widespread contamination of the environment and unwarranted degradation of grasslands and soil. BLM's Hazardous Materials Management Program attempts to mitigate only some of these problems.

As recently described by the National Research Council, the Hazardous Materials Management Program is dependent on three kinds of technology to advance its goals: advanced monitoring technologies to locate and monitor waste sites, technology to clean up hazardous substances, and technology to manage hazardous materials.[74] Many of these technologies and the strategies for using them are available from the private sector or other government agencies. BLM should take advantage of these capabilities, and those of other agencies, in developing its waste management, land use, biological resources management, and monitoring programs.

DEPARTMENT OF AGRICULTURE

■ *The Department of Agriculture should continue to strengthen its environmental R&D by following the recommendations recently made by the National Research Council and the congressional Office of Technology Assessment that call for a substantial increase in funding for competitive research grants and for a more structured, integrated, and coordinated R&D planning system.*

USDA has an extensive and longstanding agricultural research program, established over a century ago. It is centered in the department's Agricultural Research Service, although the Cooperative State Research Service (CSRS) and the Extension Service (ES) also carry out research or are involved in the delivery of research to end users and the practical application of research results. The agricultural research program is coupled with a far-reaching extension system that links 74 land grant universities and more than 31,000 county offices. The department's research efforts have been successful in some areas; however, environmental research and development, with the exception of soil conservation and some other programs, is a relatively recent venture.

The goal of USDA's agricultural R&D is to increase agricultural productivity. Its accomplishments are impressive and have contributed to making U.S. agricultural programs among the most productive in the world. With less than 7 percent of the world's land and less than 5 percent of the world's population, the United States' farmers produce 12.6 percent of the world's agricultural commodities (by value); one hour of farm labor produces nearly 8 times as much food and crops today as it did in 1947, output per acre is 40 percent higher today than it was in 1967, and each farmer in the United States produces enough food for a hundred people.

Today, USDA's research is increasingly concerned with the environmental consequences of farming and agricultural technology (for example, the effects on wetlands conservation of pesticide use) and USDA is conducting research in areas such as sustainable development, water quality, biotechnology, and food quality and safety. To help understand the potential effects of global climate change, ARS has become an active participant in the United States Global Change Research Program and is developing a strategic plan for assessing the long-term and short-term effects of climate change on American agriculture.

USDA research has been studied in depth by both the National

Research Council's Board on Agriculture and the Office of Technology Assessment (OTA) of the United States Congress. In 1989, the NRC issued a report, *Investing in Research: A Proposal to Strengthen the Agricultural, Food, and Environmental System*, which pointed out that agriculture productivity and environmental quality go hand-in-hand.[75] The NRC identified several issues of concern, including contamination of surface water and groundwater by natural and chemical fertilizers, pesticides, and sediment; the continued abuse of fragile and nutrient-poor soils; and suitable disposal of industrial and agricultural wastes.

The NRC panel recommended a major increase in support for research related to the contamination of surface water and groundwater by contaminants from agricultural production. It also recommended additional research on soil erosion in order to develop new ways to "estimate erosion, decrease displacement of soils by wind and water, and develop federal policies for conserving fragile lands," and expanded research programs related to the minimization of agricultural wastes, the development of new waste recycling technologies, and improved systems for ecologically safe waste disposal systems.

The NRC also called for expanding research support for agriculture, food, and the environment by $500 million annually, with the bulk of this increase supporting competitive grants administered through USDA's Competitive Research Grants Office. It proposed expanded competitive grant programs in six areas, including natural resources and the environment. This program area should focus on "fundamental structures and functions of ecosystems, biological and physical bases of sustainable production systems; minimizing soil and water losses and sustainable surface and groundwater quality; global climatic effects on agriculture, forestry, and biological diversity."

In its study, OTA concluded that broad changes in the basic organizational system of USDA are needed to improve agricultural research. It pointed out that USDA lacks a research mission statement, short-term and long-term planning, mechanisms for setting priorities, and appropriate funding. In OTA's view, the best solution for improving agricultural research is increased appropriations for research combined with a mission-oriented approach to R&D. The major components of this system include a clearly articulated, mission-oriented agricultural research and extension policy; a structured, integrated, and coordinated planning system; and a combination of formula and competitive grants.[76]

The 1992 Appropriations Committee hearings suggest that Congress has largely adopted the initiative suggested by the National Research Council. In 1992, the Cooperative State Research Service requested $125 million in research funds, of which approximately 12 percent was targeted to environmental research. However, many of the structural and organizational problems identified by OTA still exist. The Task Force endorses the conclusions and recommendations presented by the NRC and OTA and encourages USDA to take deliberate steps to continue to strengthen its environmental R&D programs.

DEPARTMENT OF ENERGY NATIONAL LABORATORIES

■ *The R&D activities of the Department of Energy National Laboratories should be evaluated to determine their potential to make future contributions to national and international environmental R&D programs.*

As recognized in the Carnegie Commission's report *E³: Organizing for Environment, Energy, and the Economy in the Executive Branch of the U.S. Government,*

> institutions must be designed to embrace environmental, energy, and economic goals harmoniously and coherently and to perform at the highest capability the functions of securing the knowledge base, assessing impacts, and formulating and implementing policies with both national and international dimensions.[77]

The Department of Energy has a large environmental R&D program, and its national laboratories have played and should continue to play a central role in the department's research activities. In keeping with the new vision called for above, the missions, organizational positions, and activities of DoE's National Laboratories should be reexamined and directed toward environmental, energy, and economic objectives.

The Department of Energy's R&D efforts are supported by several national laboratories, including Oak Ridge (in Tennessee), Argonne (in Illinois), Lawrence Livermore (in California), Los Alamos (in New Mexico), and Brookhaven (in New York). Historically, the primary mission of these laboratories has been to design and provide prototypes of nuclear weapons and reactors and to support the mission of the Department of Defense. In carrying out this mission, the laboratories have developed unique capabilities that can contribute to the nation's environmental protection efforts. For this to happen, however, fundamental operational changes will have to be made.

Some of the national laboratories already have environmental R&D programs in place. For example, Argonne National Laboratory is working in the area of land use and restoration; Brookhaven National Laboratory has conducted research in acid rain for many years and houses a significant program on greenhouse gases; Oak Ridge National Laboratory is developing advanced waste treatment technologies; and the Pacific Northwest Laboratory has developed technologies to reduce toxicity of wastes. In 1990, Lawrence Livermore National Laboratory established an Environmental Technology Program to develop and evaluate innovative technologies to aid in environmental restoration and waste management.

The national laboratories also have extensive computational facilities and the ability to undertake large-scale field research and to conduct studies of nonlinear, complex systems. These capabilities can be applied in several key environmental protection problem areas, particularly the cleanup of hazardous waste and the storage and analysis of environmental monitoring data. A Task Force of the Secretary of Energy Advisory Board (SEAB) has examined these and other issues in the context of the future of the National Laboratories and has made recommendations for programmatic changes in a recent report.[78]

Chemical and Nuclear Waste Disposal

The DoE and other federal agencies must address massive problems of chemical waste disposal. The department is also facing the daunting task of cleaning up nuclear waste not only at nuclear facilities, but also at the national laboratories themselves. The laboratories can contribute both to locating wastes through advanced seismic and electromagnetic techniques and to rendering them less dangerous. Once waste has been located, a promising approach to cleanup is bioremediation, which involves the development and deployment of microbes or bacteria that attack specific wastes, ingest them, and convert them to a less formidable threat. Although bioremediation is a useful mechanism to attack chemical wastes, it is of limited use in mitigating the radioactive waste problem, and novel methods to address this problem must be devised.

Successful implementation of bioremediation is closely coupled to an understanding of the ecology of underground life. The ecology of the large subterranean biomass is poorly understood, although some data have been developed, primarily by the petroleum industry. The national laboratories, through their experience in conducting drilling programs, coupled with their substantial expertise in molecular biology and related sciences, have the capability to analyze this important but largely unknown part of the biosphere and to conduct the research programs needed to implement operational bioremediation. The activities of the DoE laboratories in this area could do much to enhance the capabilities of other civilian and defense agencies facing massive cleanup problems.

Storage and Analysis of Environmental Monitoring Data

The national laboratories can also make important contributions to federal environmental R&D programs in the storage and analysis of environmental monitoring data. As research on global change proceeds, it will be essential to couple data from broad-coverage satellite observations with data from the more narrow coverage provided by remote sensing from the ground and from aircraft. The national laboratories have extensive experience in building and operating satellites and in reducing the data they generate. The laboratories have proven ability to design and build instruments, to integrate these instruments within spacecraft, and to design the data processing component essential to the success of a space-based mission. The extent of this experience is not widely known because these space-related efforts have been conducted in support of national security programs. While NASA undoubtedly will continue to have primary responsibility for much of the space effort supporting studies of global change, these capabilities make the national laboratories a resource for quick-reaction, opportunistic attempts to solve specific problems.

Political Challenges

The integration of the DoE national laboratories into environmental research and development programs presents difficult political challenges. First, many view the laboratories' historic mission as incompatible with environmental concerns. Moreover, since the design of nuclear weapons may continue to be the laboratories' primary mission, it could be difficult to focus the attention of top management on environmental research and development, which might be deemed a secondary or tertiary concern. Second, to date, the laboratories have achieved only partial success in developing expertise in the environmental sciences to complement their considerable expertise in engineering, physics, chemistry, and biology. Third, the laboratories tend to be most successful when solving problems that require large, coordinated efforts. While important aspects of environmental problems are of this character, many issues can be best addressed by the individual investigator working in the laboratory or by the individual modeler analyzing well-defined problems.

In spite of these potential difficulties, we believe that the national laboratories can and should devote substantially more attention to R&D supporting the nation's environmental protection objectives, and that the obstacles facing the national laboratories in making this mission transition can be surmounted. DoE has demonstrated that it can modify its mission to make important contributions to the mapping of the human genome.

Certainly it can modify its mission to address the major environmental challenges now facing the nation.

DEPARTMENT OF DEFENSE

■ *Department of Defense environment-related research and development efforts should be integrated with those of other federal departments and agencies. Alternatively, some of these activities could be transferred to environmental R&D programs within other departments and agencies.*

The Department of Defense (DoD) laboratory structure possesses significant capabilities for conducting environmental research. In fact, the department has funded natural science research targeted on environmental issues for many years. The Office of Naval Research has played a major role in developing the nation's oceanographic capabilities, and the Army, through a variety of programs, has funded important computer-based research as well as studies of the lower atmosphere. For many years, the Air Force has maintained a sizeable program in upper atmospheric research. Like the Department of Energy, however, the Department of Defense is responsible for a substantial proportion of the nation's hazardous waste, and it has, until recently, devoted few resources to this problem.

Environmental research within the Department of Defense is, as it should be, highly mission-oriented. However, new opportunities are developing for the department to contribute directly to the research activities of civilian federal agencies. DoD is facing major cleanup problems at its bases and installations. Research directed at solving these problems should contribute as well to the national hazardous waste cleanup effort centered in EPA's Superfund activities. The Defense Department also faces the major task of disposing of old chemical weapons, and the development of technologies to deal with obsolete highly toxic substances will have applicability to the disposal of other hazardous waste. In addition, the services and various agencies of the Defense Department have recently begun to focus on ways to minimize waste. Here again, technologies, procedures, and manufacturing systems that conserve resources could be shared with the civilian agencies.

Future environmental protection efforts will depend heavily on monitoring and mapping systems. The Defense Mapping Agency produces databases on topography that are essential to the implementation of geographic information systems. Similar databases are vital to addressing many environmental concerns. Defense databases could be expanded and, in some cases, integrated with those of civilian agencies to enhance national and international environmental monitoring efforts.

The recently initiated Strategic Environmental Research and Development Program (SERDP) presents new opportunities for further development of research and technology within the Defense Department. SERDP is intended to bring the department's technological capabilities to bear on environmental problems. Initially, most funds will be directed toward environmental cleanup activities, but in the longer term some resources are likely to be used on problems related to global climate change.

As a key component of the SERDP, the U.S. Army Corps of Engineers plays an important environmental R&D role at DoD. The Corps also maintains an active wetlands study. The Office of Naval Research in the Department of the Navy supports a sizeable basic research program, particularly in the oceanography area. It devotes about $500 million per year to research related to such subjects as tides, meteorology, and ocean pollution.

In pursuit of its mission, the Defense Department has contributed to the development of remotely piloted vehicles (RPVs), which can be employed in a variety of atmospheric studies. RPVs can provide a critically needed adjunct to satellite-based remote sensing by maintaining continuous observations at critical altitudes such as the tropopause, where satellites are less effective. In addition, RPVs can conduct *in situ* sampling. This capability could yield information on the abundance and nature of aerosols, which strongly influence the radiative balance within the atmosphere and play a key role in cloud formation.

The integration of the Defense Department's environmental research and technology development programs into the federal environmental R&D effort requires improved coordinating mechanisms. At present, the civilian agencies are unfamiliar with DoD's capabilities. By requiring the Departments of Defense and Energy to develop joint programs in consultation with the Environmental Protection Agency, the SERDP has taken a step toward achieving this more effective collaboration. Both the Office of Science and Technology Policy and the Office of Environmental Quality can contribute to the coordination process by analyzing DoD capabilities and looking for areas of potential interaction with the R&D programs of civilian agencies. It would be useful to examine whether some DoD programs might operate more effectively under other departments and agencies.

HAZARDOUS WASTE R&D

▪ *A larger proportion of the funds devoted to the cleanup of hazardous waste at federal facilities should be directed to research and development.*

In fiscal year 1992 alone, $4.3 billion was directed to environmental restoration and waste management at atomic weapons production facilities.

Yet very little of this money was earmarked for research and development. The consequence of this shortsighted policy is that tremendous opportunities to learn from the cleanup process are being lost. We believe that a substantially larger percentage of environmental restoration and waste management funds should be directed to R&D. This proportionally small investment can lead to major improvements in our understanding of the impacts of wastes on the environment and in the development of technologies to aid in waste cleanup.

Hazardous waste remediation efforts at federal facilities should be coordinated with the EPA Superfund Innovative Technologies (SITE) program and other federal efforts. In addition, a comprehensive comparative analysis of federal facility cleanup funding ($9.4 billion in federal support for FY 93) and Superfund cleanup program funding ($1.7 billion in federal support in FY 93) should be undertaken to determine if the current 5:1 ratio of support for these activities is appropriate.

6
LINKING AND COORDINATING PROGRAMS

Because of the global nature of many environmental problems, U.S. environmental R&D programs must operate in concert with those of other nations. Industrialized countries must share the burden of finding innovative solutions to the challenges of today and tomorrow. Furthermore, the federal environmental R&D effort will operate most effectively if it is linked closely with complementary programs in academia, nongovernmental organizations, and industry. The recommendations that follow suggest ways to improve these interactions—both national and international.

■ **In order to strengthen the link between environmental R&D and policy development, assessment capabilities across federal agencies should be expanded. Furthermore, U.S. environmental R&D programs should be coupled more closely with those of other nations. Greater cooperation among scientific disciplines and among federal, nongovernmental, and industrial research programs should be encouraged.**

STRENGTHENING LINKAGES

■ *The linkages between environmental R&D and policy development should be strengthened, and the federal government should substantially increase its support of multidisciplinary policy studies and assessments designed to forge and evaluate these linkages.*

The development of effective environmental policy requires interaction among the natural sciences, economics, political science, and law, among others. To date, legal considerations have dominated policy development. Lawyers have codified their interpretation of the results of natural science research into various legal prescriptions both in statutes and in regulations. At certain stages, the economic consequences of these prescriptions are examined, but often in a cursory and *post hoc* way. Social and political considerations are weighed only at the very end of the process, when laws must be passed or regulations issued and adopted.

Currently, federal agencies are focusing their environmental R&D efforts on the natural sciences. There has been minimal support for research on the economic, political, social, and legal implications of environmental issues. An even smaller fraction of R&D funds has been directed to studies that examine the interconnections between these various disciplines and the ways in which they can be enhanced. Yet investigating alternatives, raising issues, and developing new conceptual approaches to address them are all important ingredients in developing a framework for environmental policy. At present, no single institution has directed funding authority to pursue these avenues of multidisciplinary research, although such studies do proceed in a few places throughout the United States and abroad, primarily with the support of private foundations.

Federal officials and their staff have little time to consider complex policy issues and to devise alternative strategies to address them. Translating research results in the natural sciences into effective environmental policy requires the capability to link the natural sciences with economics, political science, and law. A prerequisite for developing this capability is the assurance of stable and adequate funding. We recommend that the federal government devote a larger percentage of total environmental R&D dollars to policy research and assessment, including studies of the economic, social, legal, and political aspects of environmental problems; regional, national, and international perspectives should be taken into account. These studies should be undertaken within or through the proposed Institute for Environmental Assessment, described above (page 59), as well as through the policy evaluation offices of departments and agencies, with major funding devoted to support extramural studies in academic and nongovernmental institutions.

INTERNATIONAL COOPERATION

■ *The United States should couple its environmental research and development efforts more closely with those of other nations.*

It is in the interest of the United States to develop more effective R&D collaborations with other nations in order to achieve environmental goals. In some R&D areas other nations have extensive experience in addressing certain problems, and we can learn from their efforts. Other nations have limited environmental R&D activities and can learn from our programs. The U.S. Agency for International Development (AID) supports environmental programs, some of them R&D programs, in more than 90 countries at a level of more than $400 million per year.[78] Total U.S. assistance for economic, humanitarian, environmental, and development purposes was more than $11 billion in 1991.[79]

How can the United States encourage other nations to use newer, innovative technologies, especially where older, less environmentally sound technologies are currently in use? Can a system be devised to share technology and to foster collaborative R&D efforts? Can the international R&D community work together to devise indicators of environmental quality and programs to monitor these indicators? Certain scientific disciplines are already forging international relationships to answer these kinds of questions. How can we encourage such interactions in other scientific disciplines? These are some of the important questions facing policymakers.

INVOLVEMENT OF INTERNATIONAL ORGANIZATIONS

International agencies, including the United Nations Environment Program and specialized agencies such as the World Meteorological Organization, as well as key nongovernmental scientific organizations, are promoting a range of international collaborative R&D efforts. The International Program on Chemical Safety within the World Health Organization (WHO), for example, provides updated assessments of the health risks posed by important toxic substances, aids in research and training coordination, and disseminates information world wide. WHO programs like this make important contributions to public health throughout the world and should be strongly supported by the United States. The National Institute of Environmental Health Sciences (NIEHS) makes a substantial annual contribution to this program, but this level of support may be reduced in the future.

Another example of international collaboration is the International Conference on an Agenda of Science for Environment and Development into the 21st Century (ASCEND 21). Sponsored by the International Council of Scientific Unions (ICSU), in cooperation with other nongovernmental organizations, ASCEND 21 stressed the importance of a new international partnership in environmental research and underscored the importance of the precautionary principle. This principle calls for avoiding disturbances of earth systems because of the potential for unexpected consequences when altering poorly understood systems. ASCEND agreed on the nature of major global environmental challenges and identified several high-priority areas for cooperative international research. These include population and per capita resource consumption; depletion of agricultural/land resources; inequity and poverty; climate change; loss of biological diversity; industrialization and waste; water scarcity; and energy consumption.[80] But the program has encountered difficulties because of the international politics of big versus little, developing versus developed, and North versus South. We believe that the United States should actively support programs of this kind and help them to reach their full potential. We believe the United States should play a leadership role in furthering cooperative international research efforts such as those outlined in ASCEND 21.

U.S. ROLE

Senators Gore and Domenici recently introduced legislation that would establish a program through the DoE national laboratories to assist foreign countries in addressing global energy and environmental issues.[81] Federal programs of this kind are useful in promoting the diffusion of environmental technologies to developing countries, where they can significantly influence energy conservation and environmental protection efforts.

The European Community (EC) has sponsored initiatives to improve the use of environmental technologies. We believe that the United States should collaborate with the EC countries and with academic institutions to develop and share new technologies. Involving U.S. representatives, and particularly representatives of federal agencies, with the EC effort may be a way to initiate collaborations. An effort to establish collaborative arrangements between the national laboratories of various countries would be especially worthwhile.

We endorse the recommendations of the recent Carnegie Commission report *International Environmental Research and Assessment: Proposals for Better Organization and Decision Making*. It proposes that

> the United States Government and its scientific and engineering communities should take the lead in further building the international institutional frameworks for environmental research and for advice to governments on which all nations are bound to come to rely.[82]

This would involve two major initiatives. The first is the establishment of an international consultative group for research on environment to review progress in environmental research in relation to developing countries, to improve research for these countries, and to enhance the effectiveness of research institutions by promoting cooperation between them; and the second is an improvement in the international scientific assessment of environmental issues and the integration of this assessment more effectively with international policymaking. Improved links between assessment and policymaking would involve strengthening cooperation between international scientific and technical organizations. It would also mean developing stronger ties between U.S. Government agencies that give science policy advice and their counterparts in other nations.

In an effort to improve the international links between environmental assessment and policymaking, the International Council of Scientific Unions is promoting the organization of a group of nongovernmental international and national agencies to assess environmental problems. The group would undertake assessments and meet regularly with representatives of government agencies to appraise R&D priorities and to consider approaches to achieve international environmental protection and sustainable development objectives.

THE UNITED STATES AS A RELIABLE PARTNER

The United States must work to improve its reputation as a reliable partner in international environmental efforts and must reestablish its leadership role in setting environmental policy. While other nations, such as Japan, the Netherlands, and Germany, have placed an emphasis on sustainable development, U.S. policies have lagged. U.S. governmental agencies must devote more attention to the sustainable use of resources and must direct substantially greater resources to addressing global environmental challenges through international R&D activities. One reason for establishing a new Department of the Environment is that such a department could provide leadership for U.S. governmental agencies in addressing global environmental problems while acting as a focal point for linking our environmental R&D efforts with those of other nations.

Becoming a more reliable partner in environmental efforts will also require a change in the posture of the United States Government toward international scientific cooperation. A recent study of the U.S. role in cooperating with the industrialized democracies on science and technology found that cooperation was hampered by two major factors: the lack of a coherent policy by the U.S. Government or its specific agencies toward international scientific cooperation, and the low priority accorded to international cooperation in science by the government.[83] Both of these barriers can be overcome by strong leadership.

MULTIDISCIPLINARY COMMUNICATION AND COLLABORATION

■ *Communication and collaboration between the ecological and the environmental health research communities should be enhanced in order to evaluate and address environmental problems in an integrated fashion.*

There is a significant lack of communication between health-oriented and ecology-oriented researchers and policymakers in the United States. Individuals in these fields have earned their degrees in different schools or colleges; they attend different specialty meetings, and they publish in different journals. The two groups communicate using different technical terms and are funded by different agencies. They are interested in different statutes and regulatory regimes, and, unfortunately, they seldom interact.

EFFORTS TO PROMOTE INTERACTION

This lack of interaction is detrimental to our national environmental R&D efforts. In recent years, however, there have been some promising efforts to foster interaction between these communities. In the landmark reports *Unfinished Business*[84] and *Reducing Risks*,[85] the EPA Science Advisory Board looked across the full range of risks that fall within EPA's domain. Unfortunately, the risks were ranked according to the conventional health and ecological categories. Nevertheless, we believe that the recommendation of the Advisory Board to raise ecology to the level of attention and visibility of health is an excellent beginning.

The Ecological Society of America has launched an ambitious research plan of its own, the "Sustainable Biosphere Initiative," a framework for the acquisition, dissemination, and utilization of ecological knowledge that supports efforts to ensure the sustainability of the biosphere. The framework calls for coordinated research effort focused on global change, biological diversity, and sustainable ecological systems. The initiative also calls for "a significant increase in interdisciplinary interactions that link ecologists with the broad scientific community, with mass media and educational organizations, and with policymakers and resource managers in all sectors of society."[86]

Within the National Institutes of Health, NIEHS has pursued its mission of basic research in environmental health by funding research on any animal species in which fundamental mechanisms can be studied. Thus, the NIEHS portfolio of studies is fairly broad. In some projects, particularly the Superfund Basic Research Program Projects, NIEHS has brought together highly interdisciplinary groups for both ecological and health investigations. The research tools used by these groups may be applied to both areas. The Executive Committee of the National Toxicology Program consists of the senior administrators of the National Institutes of Health, the National Cancer Institute, the National Institute of Environmental Health Sciences, the National Institute for Occupational Safety and Health, the Agency for Toxic Substances and Disease Registry, the National Center for Toxicological Research, the Food and Drug Administration, and the Environmental Protection Agency. This could serve as a useful forum for evaluating environmental problems related to human health.

The National Research Council's Board on Environmental Studies and Toxicology has an explicit mandate to address environmental and environmental health problems and has made considerable progress in doing so over the past three years. Among many other reports, NRC has issued a series of "biomarkers" studies dealing with exposure, susceptibility, and adverse effects. These reports have focused on biomarkers of reproductive and developmental toxicity, pulmonary toxicity, neurotoxicity, and immunotoxicity, as well as the effects of pollution on trees. The NRC has also been heavily involved in ecological, physical, and socioeconomic assessments of proposed offshore drilling sites. Nevertheless, finding common ground on specific projects remains a challenge.

PROMISING AREAS—RISK AND GLOBAL CLIMATE CHANGE

We believe that there are several promising areas in which greater interaction between the health and ecological communities should be pursued. The risk-assessment/risk-characterization paradigm can be applied to both ecological and health problems or potential problems. Identification of hazard, characterization of risk, and reduction of exposure and risk are common activities, as is the overarching challenge of risk communication. The NRC has established a Committee on Risk Assessment Methodology composed of individuals from the health and ecological research communities who are working together to develop methodologies to assess the risks posed by a broad range of environmental problems.

The global climate change problem has brought environmental modelers and toxicologists together. Stratospheric ozone depletion has been linked primarily to an increased incidence of skin cancer in human beings as a consequence of higher ultraviolet radiation exposure. However, effects on plankton and other components of the environment may also be significant. When scientific evidence is brought together for risk assessment and risk management purposes, it is essential to understand both the health and the ecological benefits of exposure reduction. Otherwise, only some of the benefits of proposed regulatory actions will be recognized, while the full costs of these actions will receive primary attention.

BUILDING BRIDGES BETWEEN ECOLOGY AND HEALTH

There are opportunities for federal agencies and for Congress to build more bridges between ecological and health research programs. One approach is to foster interdisciplinary programs in federal agencies and in academic institutions. For example, the University of Washington's Institute for Environmental Studies brings together faculty members from the ecological and health communities to work on problems of common interest. We believe that other academic institutions should pursue similar multidisciplinary arrangements.

Second, federal agencies should develop requests for proposals (RFPs) that require interdisciplinary efforts to address environmental problems. Making federal funds available on this basis provides a powerful incentive for investigators and research programs to forge collaborative working relationships. A third approach is for Congress and the Executive Office of the President to encourage interactions between federal agencies and programs that are addressing different aspects of environmental problems. To some extent, the Federal Coordinating Council on Science, Engineering, and Technology within the Office of Science and Technology Policy develops *ad hoc* interactions of this kind, but we believe that additional, more permanent interagency linkages should be sought. For example, EPA's Health Effects Research Laboratory and the National Institute of Environmental Health Sciences, both in Research Triangle Park, North Carolina, should develop collaborative research programs, as noted on pages 81–82. Federal agencies should link their programs and exchange personnel more frequently to foster such collaborations.

LINKS WITH NONGOVERNMENTAL ORGANIZATIONS

■ *The environmental research and policymaking linkages between federal agencies and nongovernmental organizations should be strengthened.*

Nongovernmental environmental organizations (NGOs) occupy a unique niche in the policymaking community.[87] Because most of them operate independently of government and industry, they are in a position to undertake critical evaluation of existing policies and to present alternatives. Insulated from the more immediate pressures that drive federal and state agencies, NGOs are able to offer a longer-range perspective and continuity of thinking to policy planning. They can be a significant force in breaking policy gridlock by functioning as "bridging institutions," organizations that can circumvent obstacles, resolve disputes, and catalyze consensus building.[88]

In pursuing their goals, environmental NGOs may or may not operate in an advocacy context. Some organizations do not take public positions on political issues. Others are politically active, entering the fray in an effort to influence policy development in various ways and to increase their membership and enhance their visibility. The activities of most environmental NGOs fall somewhere in between these two poles of political involvement. With respect to scientific questions, the nonadvocacy NGOs have some advantages in that the credibility of their work is not called into question because of political leanings. Such credibility is particularly important for organizations that maintain specialized scientific expertise.

NGOs' Contribution to Policymaking

Over the years, a number of NGOs have made major contributions to national environmental policy. Resources for the Future pioneered much of the early thinking on economics and the environment, proposing the use of economic incentive-based approaches to achieving environmental quality objectives. The Conservation Foundation and the World Wildlife Fund have been particularly successful in dispute resolution and in building a consensus among diverse outside groups with respect to policy initiatives. The "no net loss in wetlands" policy goal resulted from this type of effort. The World Resources Institute has played a key role in the area of global climate change and technology policy, and the Environmental Law Institute is a leader in the analysis of the judicial and regulatory aspects of policy issues. Several other NGOs make important contributions to environmental policymaking in a range of different ways.

NGOs may be organized in response to specific governmental needs. The Health Effects Institute (HEI), established in 1980 and jointly funded by government and industry, works to develop the "credible facts" required to make reasoned policy decisions with respect to the regulation of automobile emissions. The HEI–Asbestos Research was established in 1988 in response to a request to HEI from Congress to try to resolve the controversy about the health risks posed by asbestos in buildings. And Clean Sites, Inc., was established in 1983 to "accelerate the cleanup execution" at Superfund hazardous waste sites.[89]

The independence, specialized skills, and consensus-building abilities of the NGOs are particularly useful in the policymaking process. Because it is difficult to replicate these qualities within federal and state agencies, government agencies should establish and strengthen formal and informal contacts with NGOs. Contracts and grants are two common formal arrangements; representatives of NGOs interact with federal officials by serving on advisory panels or by providing periodic advice on a consulting basis. However, exchange of data and other information is the most common kind of informal interaction.

STRENGTHENING THE LINKAGES

The linkages between NGOs and governmental agencies could be strengthened in several ways. Increased funding for competitive grants and contracts in the policy analysis and development area would give governmental units greater access to NGO expertise. Federal extramural funding for policy analysis is currently very limited; and it should be expanded substantially. Also, governmental organizations should take greater advantage of the capabilities of NGOs if they were more aware of the expertise that exists within key organizations. To this end, NGOs could support the production of a guide for government officials and others informing them of the analytical capabilities and expertise of the major policy-oriented environmental organizations.

Finally, one or more of the environmental NGOs (including professional societies) should work with the American Association for the Advancement of Science (AAAS) to undertake an annual governmentwide analysis and critique of federal environmental research budgets. Such an analysis would be useful to analysts both within and outside the federal government. AAAS has already undertaken an analysis of federal environmental R&D budgets for the National Research Council and the Carnegie Commission.[90] We encourage the continuation of this effort.

LINKS WITH INDUSTRY

■ *Environmental R&D programs within the federal government and industry should be linked more closely, and the federal government should continue to provide incentives for environmental R&D efforts in industry in order to advance common goals.*

There are many areas in which industrial environmental research and development efforts are aligned with those of the federal government. There are also many areas that are not interconnected, and need not be.

Most of the new technology required for new, low-waste/no-waste technologies can be developed by industry without government support. However, some government assistance is needed to encourage exploratory or general technology development.

DIFFERENT CULTURES, DIFFERENT INCENTIVES

Government and industry laboratories operate in very different cultures and are driven by different incentives. This is especially true of environmental abatement and remediation activities. Industry has many incentives to expedite such work, including community relations, financial expediency, and internal corporate goals. Government, on the other hand, acts in response to mandates from policymakers in the executive and legislative branches.

Each federal laboratory aspires to have, and many claim to have, expertise in several areas of environmental research. However, these research programs are often not well focused, and coordination of laboratory programs is weak. In addition, some government researchers and laboratories are more interested in working on "new technology" and "process development," rather than abatement. Yet, abatement-related R&D is a high-priority need. Government and industry researchers must identify high-priority abatement problems and opportunities to work cooperatively and share information.

To date, too few comprehensive technology assessments have been conducted to support efforts to define goals and establish budget priorities. In addition, even when excellent technology assessments have been undertaken by objective professionals, a consensus on the conclusions and recommendations is hard to forge because the affected parties have different economic, social, and philosophical interests.

Industry and government laboratories alike are heavily focused on the "easy" solutions to environmental R&D efforts, and there is little incentive to expand R&D efforts to tackle more difficult challenges. A plethora of problems is facing the nation, some of which are naturally easier to solve than others. Moreover, researchers typically are working on such a small part of the huge environmental puzzle that they frequently do not recognize findings of significance to other scientific disciplines. They find it difficult to pursue tangential findings or address needs that may become evident during the research and development process.

MERITS AND MECHANISMS OF COOPERATION

A more cooperative spirit appears to be emerging within federal agencies and industries, a spirit that could be translated into joint or cooperative

R&D strategies. To foster communication between government and industry laboratories, we encourage the establishment of informal strategy forums designed to bring together representatives of industry and government. A neutral third party, such as one of the professional societies, the National Research Council, or the Government–University–Industry Research Round-table, may be helpful in identifying opportunities for information exchange and strategic planning. In some cases, a government laboratory may be able to serve as a forum and technology broker.

Joint government–industry demonstration efforts can be particularly useful in showing how innovative technologies can be applied in the industrial setting. Partnerships of this kind can help bridge related government and industry R&D efforts and promote the transfer and diffusion of technologies within the industrial sector.

The American Institute of Chemical Engineers (AIChE) Center for Waste Reduction Technologies provides an industry focus for policy questions in this area. The center offers an opportunity for groups of companies to work together to advance the development of waste reduction technologies. However, AIChE influences only a narrow cross-section of industry, albeit a critical one. The institute could build alliances with other professional organizations to expand its base. One possibility is to interact with the Society of Manufacturing Engineers, which is awakening to the challenges of environmental protection. Likewise, EPA's Superfund Innovative Technology Evaluation program can serve both as a forum and as a technology broker. An industry-led initiative aimed at cooperation with the SITE program and with EPA's Office of Research and Development could be very productive as well.

We believe that joint government–industry R&D efforts should emphasize consolidation of development efforts without sacrificing the potential for generation of new initiatives that the existence of many sources offers. Such efforts should also identify potential technology bridges to promote the free exchange of information between the principal investigator for an initiative at a federal laboratory and the comparable initiative leader in industry; cooperative policy planning exercises should also be undertaken. Industrial organizations such as the Petroleum Environmental Forum, the AIChE Center for Waste Reduction Technologies, and similar groups in the aircraft and automotive industries should seek new opportunities to interact with government scientists and engineers.

Joint industry–government technology assessments would be worthwhile in certain areas such as economic and technical performance metrics. Efforts such as these help to identify emerging technologies and define new technology needs.

7
BUILDING A STRONG INTELLECTUAL BASE

Implicit in all of our recommendations up to this point is the assumption that there must be a pool of highly trained professionals to carry out the research and development activities that are critical to our environmental protection programs. Yet this assumption may be little more than wishful thinking in the absence of strong programs and facilities for basic research, education, and training.

■ **The science and technology base that underpins our environmental R&D programs must be strengthened to ensure the availability of environmental scientists and engineers, social scientists, and policy analysts, and to ensure adequate facilities and equipment to support their work.**

NATIONAL SCIENCE FOUNDATION

■ *The National Science Foundation and other government agencies should take steps to strengthen the base upon which our national environmental R&D programs are built.*

The scope and direction of grant programs in NSF and other agencies that support environmental R&D activities in universities, nongovernmental organizations, and elsewhere should be examined carefully to determine if additional funding is needed to support certain kinds of research activities. NSF plays an essential role in ensuring that the United States has the scientific disciplinary base necessary to support the nation's future environmental R&D needs. Its experience in awarding federal grants based on merit review procedures makes it an appropriate agency for supporting extramural environmental research activities.

We believe that NSF should substantially expand extramural grants programs devoted to policy research, particularly research designed to integrate the thinking across multiple disciplines (for example, energy, environment, and economics; environmental health and economics; law, regulatory strategies, and risk analysis). NSF should pay particular attention to the adequacy of the nation's environmental science and technology disciplinary base. Certain disciplines, such as environmental biology, will require additional support as the nation and the world strive to achieve sustainable development. The National Research Council's Committee on Environmental Research is evaluating research and development opportunities and needs with respect to protecting the environment. Their conclusions will be useful in identifying other areas that require more federal support.

In addition, NSF, with the assistance of the National Research Council, should undertake a study of the future environmental R&D manpower needs of the nation. In response to the findings and recommendations of this study, NSF should expand existing and establish new competitive educational programs designed to train the physical, biological, and social scientists, engineers, and policy analysts of the future. NSF should work with other federal agencies, especially the Environmental Protection Agency (or a new Department of the Environment), and leading investigators throughout the nation to identify priority research needs and to direct resources toward them.

IMPROVING EDUCATION

■ *Both government and the private sector should take deliberate steps to improve educational programs in the environmental sciences.*

Undergraduate biological, physical, engineering, business, and economics educational programs should include an environmental science component in their curricula. Environmental issues cut across nearly all disciplines; consequently, a broad range of academic courses should have environmental components. Interdisciplinary studies courses are also needed to give students a broad understanding of environmental problems and to train them in the area of environmental policy.

Graduate and postdoctoral training programs in the environmental and social sciences should be expanded. Additional natural resource economists, environmental health professionals, and risk analysts, among others, will be needed in the future. Several universities have initiated undergraduate programs in environmental studies that combine disciplines such as biology, earth science, engineering, and economics.[91] Programs of this kind should be developed in a larger number of universities throughout the nation to ensure a sufficient pool of trained individuals to meet the future personnel needs of industry and government, as well as the anticipated demand for university-level researchers and professors and secondary-school teachers.

8

CONCLUSION:
KNOWLEDGE AND LEADERSHIP FOR THE FUTURE

The recent United Nations Conference on Environment and Development in Rio de Janeiro focused the attention of world governments and the international public on the new and continuing threats to our global environment. The agreements achieved at that Earth Summit are steps in the right direction, but the meeting also served to highlight just how serious the continuing threats to the biosphere are and how massive and complex the task of overcoming them will be.

KNOWLEDGE AND PROGRESS

Solving the problems highlighted at the conference — the decrease in biodiversity, global climate change, the pressure of growing global population on forests, freshwater supplies, and food, and many more — will require huge outlays of capital and resources. Some environmentalists believe that a restructuring of the global economy will be necessary to respond to these challenges.[92] But a redistribution of existing resources will be insufficient without major increases in knowledge. This is why the U.S. role in environmental R&D is critically important, and why it is necessary to improve the way the federal government does environmental R&D.

The recommendations made in this report can help the federal government improve its R&D programs; they will also enable the nation to apply the resulting information effectively to the urgent environmental problems the world faces.

SUPPORTING AGENCY MISSIONS

If adopted, our recommendations would strengthen the contributions of environmental R&D to the missions of federal departments and agencies. For example, the consolidation of laboratories and the establishment of new research centers would make EPA more effective; the expansion of training programs at NIEHS would enhance NIH's role in environmental health; better planning and coordination of research, as well as changes in the Park Service and the Bureau of Land Management, would help the Department of the Interior protect our public lands and waterways; the changes we have recommended at the Department of Agriculture would help that agency fulfill its missions, because agricultural productivity and environmental quality go hand in hand. Our recommendations would also help the Department of Defense shift away from its Cold War preoccupation with the Soviet threat to a broader definition of security, and help the Department of Energy with the massive cleanup of hazardous waste at nuclear facilities.

ASSESSMENT, STRATEGIC PLANNING, AND
POLICY DEVELOPMENT

We have stressed throughout this report that federal environmental R&D is fragmented and overly focused on short-term problems. To generate the knowledge needed to meet the threats to our planet, the federal system will require better assessment, strategic planning, and policy development capabilities. In particular, the system needs a central coordinating mechanism that can assess problems, develop policy options, set priorities, and shift our R&D system away from short-range, end-of-the-pipe solutions and toward identifying trends, finding root causes, and anticipating problems.

Many federal departments and agencies have environmental R&D programs, and the goals and content of these programs vary widely. It is for this reason that we have recommended bringing all federal environmental R&D programs under one management umbrella, through an Environmental Research and Monitoring Initiative. The Initiative would help the President, through the Office of Environmental Quality, the OSTP, and key agency administrators, set goals and devise strategies to achieve them. We also believe that the enhanced roles we have recommended for the OSTP and the OEQ would strengthen the policy process. In addition, to shift the focus away from the short-term and to strengthen coordination, we have recommended changes in individual departments and agencies and have suggested ways in which these organizations can work together more closely.

Ultimately, of course, focusing and coordinating the federal environmental R&D effort will have an impact only if it leads to new policies. A new Institute for Environmental Assessment would undertake its own analyses and support the work of individuals and institutions outside the federal government through contracts and grants. The Institute would help to ensure that research in the natural and social sciences is brought into the policy arena in the executive branch, much as the Office of Technology Assessment brings together technology and policy for Congress. This new institute, of course, is no guarantee that good policies will be adopted, but we believe that it will be an invaluable resource for bridging the gap that now exists between research and policy.

BETTER MONITORING AND INFORMATION STORAGE

One of the first requirements for creating new knowledge about the environment is a system that can monitor the ongoing natural and human-induced changes in the biosphere. To be useful, information derived from monitoring—especially environmental statistics—must be stored in a form that makes it readily available to those making policy assessments and decisions. Our recommendations will improve the gathering and use of information in several ways.

A new Environmental Monitoring Agency (EMA), combining the National Oceanic and Atmospheric Administration, the U.S. Geological Survey, and some programs within EPA, would bring the key federal environmental monitoring activities together under one roof. The EMA would also work to guide and strengthen the coordination of the environmental monitoring efforts of NASA and other agencies. The National Center for Environmental Information, to be established as part of the EMA, would be a focal point for the storage and retrieval of environmental data.

MAINTAINING A STRONG SCIENCE AND TECHNOLOGY BASE

We recognize that the federal environmental R&D effort will not be able to create new knowledge and apply it to the problems the world faces over time unless it rests on a strong intellectual base. Ultimately, the federal effort will founder without a continuing supply of well-trained natural and social scientists, engineers, health professionals, policy analysts, and others. By strengthening training institutions, helping them communicate with each other and with government and industry, and promoting interdisciplinary training, the recommendations made here can help to provide the environmental experts we need.

CREATING LINKAGES

Our recommendations would also help produce new knowledge by creating new links between environmental researchers. For example, we have recommended linking our national environmental efforts much more closely with international efforts at the United Nations, the European Community, and elsewhere. A closer working relationship would help the United States learn from other nations, help the United States provide assistance to nations whose environmental efforts lag behind ours, and strengthen the bonds of cooperation that are increasingly necessary for the solution of the environmental problems we now confront.

We have also called for the establishment of a new grant program, new forms of collaboration, and new informal forums to link the federal effort more closely with key research efforts outside government—at academic institutions, nongovernmental organizations, and industrial environmental R&D programs.

Moreover, many of our recommendations would strengthen interdisciplinary collaboration on environmental R&D both inside the federal government and outside it, bringing the environmental health, social science, and engineering communities together with the ecological community. This is especially important because a reliance on the traditional disciplines of natural and physical science will not be sufficient to overcome the challenges of the future. To cite but one example, the federal government can no longer afford to consider environmental and economic issues separately. In the words of one expert in this area,

> Global warming is a form of feedback from the earth's ecological system to the world's economic system. So are the ozone hole, acid rain in Europe and

eastern North America, soil degradation in the prairies, deforestation and species loss in the Amazon, and many other environmental phenomena.[93]

We have recommended, therefore, that the federal government foster multidisciplinary programs in federal agencies and academic programs. In particular, we believe that a larger percentage of the total federal environmental R&D budget should be devoted to interdisciplinary policy research.

Finally, many of our recommendations are intended to strengthen the links between federal agencies, whose environmental R&D programs tend to be isolated from each other. For example, many of the changes we have called for in EPA laboratories would help coordinate their activities. We have also called for closer links between NASA's environmental monitoring activities and those of other federal agencies, for closer ties between NIEHS and EPA's health research program, for an integration of DoE laboratories into environmental R&D programs, and for closer connections between DoD and other agencies doing environmental research.

THE IMPORTANCE OF LEADERSHIP

Our recommendations cover a wide range of areas—from the missions of individual government agencies to reform of school curricula—because the need for change is great and the environmental problems we face are urgent. We would stress, however, that the many important problems that the federal environmental R&D effort faces do not stem from a lack of talented people or resources. The recommendations we have made for funding increases and new personnel are modest in comparison to the past R&D expenditures made at the DoE national laboratories, for example. What the federal environmental R&D effort needs most urgently is leadership—leadership to direct the talents of scientists, engineers, and others throughout the nation toward well-defined objectives.

THE PARADOX OF PROGRESS

We live in a time of paradox. Never in history have so many people had access to so much knowledge, such advanced technology, and so many resources. Yet billions of people live in poverty, and in some regions of the world living standards are falling, not rising. Never in history have so many people known so much about the dangers to our environment, or had so much knowledge that could be used to improve it. Yet population growth and increasing consumption of resources have led to deforestation and watershed destruction throughout the world, have destroyed species, have changed the atmosphere in potentially serious ways, have increased vulnerability to extreme natural events, and have posed difficult problems in managing solid and toxic wastes.

The only way to resolve these dilemmas is through sustainable development that meets the needs of present generations without jeopardizing the well-being of future ones. Such development will be possible only with major advances in knowledge that will allow us to use our resources more efficiently without damaging the environment. The United States must take the lead in pursuing such knowledge, but it can do so only if the federal research effort is reformed.

APPENDIXES

APPENDIX A
FEDERAL ENVIRONMENTAL R&D PROGRAMS

ENVIRONMENTAL PROTECTION AGENCY

The U.S. Environmental Protection Agency (EPA) is the federal government's single largest regulator, its rules imposing annual costs estimated at more than $80 billion.[94] EPA is also the *de facto* lead agency for environmental R&D, overseeing several programs that, taken together, comprise the largest internal environmental research effort in the federal government. Like the agency as a whole, EPA's research program has been focused primarily on regulation and regulatory support, and thus relies upon a strong program in applied research.

The Office of Research and Development (ORD) is charged with providing the information base EPA needs to carry out its regulatory mission. The $502 million appropriated for research at EPA in FY 1992 was part of a slow but steady upward trend in the research budget since the Agency's founding in 1970, the only exception being a reduction in funding between 1982 and 1984 (see Figure A.1).[95] In constant dollars, however, EPA's R&D budget has declined by about 11 percent between 1980 and 1992.

ORD is organized into eight offices and twelve field laboratories that corre-

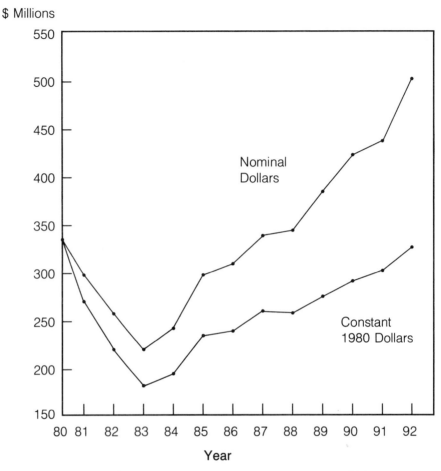

Figure A1. EPA Office of Research and Development FY 1980–1992 **Funding.** (Source: R. Gorman, Subcommittee on the Environment, Committee on Science, Space, and Technology, U.S. House of Representatives.)

spond to EPA's functional areas of research. ORD's four research strategy committees—air, water, pesticides and toxic substances, and solid waste and emergency response (Superfund)—provide overall coordination and set priorities for research. The ORD program focuses on the following environmental media: air and radiation, water quality, drinking water, pesticides and toxic substances, multimedia, hazardous waste, and Superfund. This research program includes special emphasis on global climate change, assessing environmental risks, and pollution prevention.

Within ORD, the Office of Exploratory Research (OER) coordinates a small extramural program in basic, long-term research. OER is in general responsible for informing the national academic research community about the current research challenges facing the EPA, and it backs up this mission with a research grants program and a research centers program. OER's research grants program funds individual investigators' research in areas of interest to the agency, including health, biology, chemistry and physics, and engineering. The Environmental Research Centers Program, initiated in 1979, was once a collection of twelve university-based centers, each specializing in a sustained basic science program in a single, specific area such as groundwater, marine science, or hazardous waste.[96] Today the program supports four centers.

The Office of Environmental Processes and Effects Research examines the entry, movement, and effect of pollutants across the whole range of environmental media, while the Office of Modeling, Monitoring Systems, and Quality Assurance emphasizes research in methods for environmental measurement and monitoring in the characterization, transport, and fate of ecological pollutants. The Office of Health Research's program aims to identify hazards, conduct dose–response assessments, and develop chemical-specific information for regulatory support and technical assistance. The Office of Environmental Engineering and Technology Demonstration has a research program to study, develop, and demonstrate technologies to mitigate environmental impacts, particularly in hazardous waste and waste water. Finally, the Office of Health and Environmental Assessment examines the degree of risk posed by environmental pollutants in order to provide the scientific bases for regulatory decisions and coordinating consistency in risk assessments throughout the agency.

A major challenge facing all of these offices and the entire EPA R&D program is a conflict between research to support the immediate regulatory needs of the agency and the desire to engage in a long-term program of basic environmental research. Traditionally, EPA has devoted only a small proportion of its resources to basic research.

The applied research program is an essential link in the agency's efforts to meet the requirements of an ever-growing body of environmental regulation. Designing EPA's research program to be primarily one of "fighting fires" in meeting near-term programmatic needs is not the optimal way to approach environmental protection. Instead, a more long-term, anticipatory, and prevention-oriented research program focused on basic science — that is, research aimed at a better understanding of the fundamental aspects of an environmental phenomenon as opposed to research aimed toward specific applications — should provide the foundation for assessing risk and setting priorities, for new and innovative mitigation techniques, and for technological developments leading to preventive measures. A recent study by the National Academy of Public Administration documented the nearsighted nature of EPA's research.[97]

EPA's regulatory priorities, and consequently the bulk of its research program, are dependent upon congressionally mandated appropriations, which in turn ultimately stem from public perceptions about environmental risks and the scope of environmental problems. However, the public's perceptions of risk do not coincide with those of the experts. Assessing risk requires a long-term, basic research program — something that is sorely lacking at EPA. The exploratory research grants program, for example, has been neither significant nor consistent over time, hindering many university-based researchers from conducting fundamental research that supports EPA's mission; the result is that "the base of academic research talent available to EPA is being seriously eroded rather than expanded and replenished."[98]

These kinds of problems are not unknown to the leaders within EPA. In the spring of 1992, EPA Administrator William K. Reilly testified to Congress on a report he had requested from four academic experts regarding EPA's research program.[99] The report candidly described the weaknesses of EPA's research programs, leading Administrator Reilly to cite his own concerns about the quality and direction of science at EPA and to indicate his desire to make EPA a "premiere science agency." The report called for more science advisors within the agency, a greater reliance on peer review and quality assurance programs, better career opportunities for senior scientists, the recruitment of several research scientists and engineers with world-class reputations, and improved education and outreach programs.

Despite its shortcomings, however, EPA's research program boasts some notable accomplishments. The research program mirrors the agency's regulatory program in its breadth, covering issues from the health effects of air pollution to the ecological consequences of wetlands loss, and it has been successful in supporting the crisis-oriented needs of the regulatory program. Pollution prevention activities are receiving increasing attention within ORD, as are global climate change and risk assessment.

EPA is also expanding its statistical capabilities through programs such as EMAP, the Environmental Monitoring and Assessment Program. Though subject to some early criticism of its design, EMAP is intended to further the development of environmental indicators and monitoring information by assessing the current extent and location and major ecological resources as well as their rate of deterioration.[100] Recent efforts within EPA to improve the quality of science and to renew the research mission, including a proposal to rename ORD the Office of Science and Technology, also seem promising.

NATIONAL SCIENCE FOUNDATION

The National Science Foundation (NSF) supports basic scientific and engineering research, education, and training in the environmental field through competitive grant programs. Two major divisions, covering a wide range of disciplines, funded research totaling more than $540 million in 1992, making NSF the largest source of extramural grants in the environmental field.

The Directorate for Biological Sciences funds research in biotic systems and resources, molecular biosciences, and cellular biosciences. The thrust of this program is to understand "the genetic and ecological basis for variation in the life histories and physiologies of organisms that allow them to respond to changing environments."[101] In addition, the new Directorate for Social, Behavioral, and Economic Sciences funds research that seeks to explore the anthropogenic causes and effects of ecological change. Significant funding is devoted to study of the global change phenomenon, particularly the economic effects of global change on international trade, the environmental constraints on growth in developing countries, environment-related technological change, and decision making in the public and private sectors in response to short- and long-term environmental risks.

The Directorate for Geosciences supports projects in basic research aimed at understanding and modeling earth systems. Atmospheric sciences, earth sciences, ocean sciences, and arctic and antarctic research are among specific areas of focus. Work in these areas includes understanding the weather and climate variations, groundwater supplies and quality, nuclear waste disposal capabilities, and ocean drilling. The largest portion of the division's resources is devoted to atmospheric and ocean sciences, including $51.4 million to support the National Center for Atmospheric Research in Boulder, Colorado, and a number of oceanographic centers. NSF provides about 50 percent of federal support for basic geoscience research.

NSF also houses a small extramural grants program in scientific, technological, and international affairs that funds projects in policy research and analysis and some international cooperative scientific activities.

NSF is often commended for the strong merit review system that it employs in distributing research funds. Grants are highly competitive, with only about 15 percent of proposed projects receiving funding each year. Although funds for environment-related research in the social and economic sciences have increased in recent years, these fields have not received nearly as much support as the health and physical sciences.

NATIONAL OCEANIC AND ATMOSPHERIC ADMINISTRATION

The National Oceanic and Atmospheric Administration, a division of the Commerce Department, supports an environmental research program to monitor the status and trends of the oceans and atmosphere. The research program is operated primarily through the Office of Oceanic and Atmospheric Research; supporting offices include the National Environmental Satellite Data and Information Service, the National Marine Fisheries Service, the National Ocean Service, and the National Weather Service. More than $300 million was allocated in 1992 for environment-related research at NOAA, a substantial increase over the $216 million appropriated in 1989.[102] The National Weather Service is undertaking a major modernization and restructuring program to improve its effectiveness in observing and understanding the atmosphere.[103]

Climate and global change research has become a primary focus at NOAA, much of it aimed at internationally based oceanic and atmospheric trends. The largest portion of the research effort is now centered on the U.S. Global Change Research Program; NOAA is a key agency in establishing an integrated monitoring program for measuring earth systems, for developing conceptual and predictive system models, and for maintaining a global environmental sciences data management system.

Other research programs at NOAA include coastal and ocean research targeted water quality and coastal ecosystem management; its observations and data form the basis for management decisions associated with the development, use, and protection of these resources. Solar and weather research also are components of the NOAA environmental research program. The Space Environmental Service Center and Laboratory monitor the sun and its influence on earth-based systems, and the applied atmospheric research of the National Weather Service is designed to provide accurate weather forecasting for the nation. A key component of both programs is the National Environmental Satellite, Data and Information Service, which is a system of polar-orbiting and geostationary satellites providing data both globally and regionally on ozone levels, temperature and moisture, cloud cover, and wind speed.

A significant drawback of the NOAA environmental research program, many believe, is the agency's location in the Department of Commerce. Aside from the concern that its location may incline NOAA toward providing "environmental services" to business, its relative isolation limits linkages to other agencies engaged in environmental R&D. In addition, in part because of its position in the Department of Commerce and its remoteness, NOAA has historically been vulnerable to budget cuts, especially during the early to mid-1980s (see Figure A.2). However, the recent federal global warming research initiative has helped reverse this trend.

DEPARTMENT OF ENERGY

The Department of Energy (DoE) operates a program in Biological and Environmental Research that aims to identify, understand, and anticipate the long-term health and environmental consequences of energy use. Research efforts include studies in atmospheric chemistry, a marine program to understand the exchange of energy and materials between the continental shelf and the open ocean, studies of subsurface groundwater and soil transport of energy by-products (including problems of storing and disposing of nuclear waste), studies of adverse health effects of exposure to radiation and chemicals through DoE programs, and efforts to study carbon dioxide and the global change phenomenon. These programs are carried out through the Office of Energy Research and the Fossil Energy Division; also involved are the National Environmental Research Parks and the National Laboratories system, including Argonne, Brookhaven, Berkeley, Lawrence Livermore, Los Alamos, and Oak Ridge. The National Laboratories have been instrumental in the work of the National Acid Precipitation Assessment Program. DoE devoted nearly $800 million to environmental R&D in 1992, a large portion of this supporting the development of clean coal technologies.[104]

DoE plans to devote tremendous resources to the cleanup of waste generated at federal facilities engaged in weapons research. It has been estimated that more than $150 billion will be required over the next 30 years to clean up all of the DoE facilities. Unfortunately, only a small percentage of current funding is directed to true R&D related to hazardous waste disposal and its effects on the environment. As a result, relatively little is being learned from the cleanup process.

$ Millions

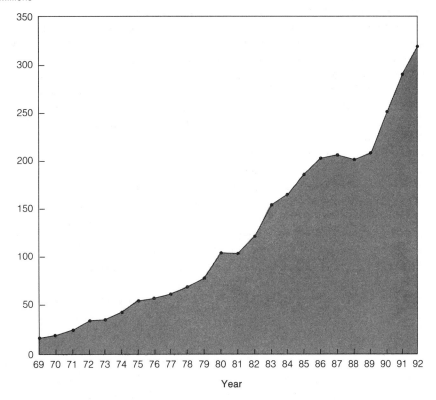

Figure A2. Funding for Environmental R&D at NOAA, 1969–1992

DoE has a critical role to play in the increasingly important linkages between environmental, energy, and economic policies. The National Laboratories are a tremendous resource of expertise and equipment, and the department is examining ways to direct more of their resources to energy and environmental R&D.

DEPARTMENT OF THE INTERIOR

As caretaker of the nation's public lands and waterways, the Department of the Interior maintains a sizeable ecological research program. Most environmental R&D at Interior is located in three of the department's five divisions, the largest programs being in the Fish and Wildlife Service, the U.S. Geological Survey, and the Minerals Management Service.

The U.S. Fish and Wildlife Service's research program provides the data and analysis "to conserve, protect, and enhance fish and wildlife and their habitats for the continuing benefit of people."[105] Through a system of 13 National Research Centers and 41 Cooperative Research Units, the environmental R&D program includes studies in contaminants, habitat protection and management, population management and restoration, and disease management. This research is particularly important in developing the Endangered and Threatened Species List. It has played a central role, for example, in the controversy over the Northern Spotted Owl and forest policy in the Northwest. Some $85 million was appropriated for environmental R&D at the Fish and Wildlife Service in 1992.

Within the Land and Minerals Management Division, the Bureau of Land Management, the Minerals Management Service, and the Office of Surface Mining have small environment-related research programs. They include work in forestry, stressed ecosystem management, and global climate change. The Minerals Management Service is responsible for oil and gas development on the outer continental shelf, and it evaluates the effects of these activities through its Environmental Studies Program. Studies of this program undertaken in recent years by the National Research Council provide several recommendations for improving research at MMS.[106]

The Water and Sciences Division conducts research through the Bureau of Reclamation, the Bureau of Mines, and the U.S. Geological Survey. The Bureau of Mines houses a research program to develop technology for treating waste from mining operations and to minimize land disturbances resulting from mining operations.

The U.S. Geological Survey's original charter charges it with the "classification of the public lands and examination of the geological structure, mineral resources, and products of the national domain."[107] Its activities include monitoring, gathering data, and conducting analyses of land resources, minerals and energy resources, and geologic hazards. It is also responsible for studies in surface water and groundwater assessment and protection, toxic and nuclear substances hydrology, acid rain, and climate change hydrology. The bulk of its program is carried out in three divisions: the National Mapping Program, Geologic Investigations, and Water Resources Investigations. USGS is also a key player in conducting monitoring activities as part of the U.S. Global Change Research Program.

NATIONAL AERONAUTICS AND SPACE ADMINISTRATION

The National Aeronautics and Space Administration (NASA) conducts a highly capital-intensive environmental research program through space-based observations of land surface, oceans, and atmosphere. The goal of the program is to gain an understanding of the entire earth system on a global, interrelated scale. In part because of the high cost of the spaceborne hardware necessary for NASA's research program, NASA devoted more than $800 million to environmental R&D in 1992.

NASA's research program examines each of the component parts of the earth system, to see how they have evolved, how they function, and how they may continue to evolve, in seeking to carry out its mission of understanding the earth from a holistic perspective. These component parts include programs in geodynamics, ocean and land processes, atmospheric dynamics and radiation, and atmospheric chemistry. The largest portion of the NASA environmental R&D budget today, however, is devoted to meeting the agency's mandates as a primary member of the U.S. Global Change Research program. NASA is the lead agency for extraterrestrial observation and support and provides critical data on atmospheric gases, land surface climatology, and ocean productivity.

Part of its effort to be a leader in environmental R&D, NASA's Earth Observing System (EOS) is an internationally coordinated, multidisciplinary spaceborne observation system that serves as the centerpiece of the agency's "Mission to Planet Earth" initiative. Mission to Planet Earth seeks to chart the processes, movements, and relationships among the earth's components as an integrated system, and it will address major environmental issues such as global warming, stratospheric ozone depletion, tropical deforestation, and desertification. EOS employs several remote sensing satellites and a data and information system in its research program. A recent report by the General Accounting office on the EOS Data and Information system is critical of early system design for lacking key advanced information management technologies that will be required for EOS data to be accessible and useful for some time in the future. The report also stresses that NASA should cooperate more closely with other federal agencies with similar data management experience and similar missions such as NOAA and NSF.[108]

DEPARTMENT OF HEALTH AND HUMAN SERVICES

Considerable research in the environmental health field is carried out through various branches of the Department of Health and Human Services (HHS). The focal point for this effort is the National Institute of Environmental Health Sciences (NIEHS) within the National Institutes of Health. NIEHS's research spans a broad range of disciplines and environmental media, and its research funding has followed a steady upward trend throughout the 1980s. The 1992 appropriation was $303 million, a large portion of which went toward sponsorship of its extramural research grants program.

NIEHS's primary mission is to "conduct and support basic biomedical research studies to identify chemical, physical, and biological environmental agents that threaten human health."[109] NIEHS has a strong program in toxicology testing, test method development, and validation. Other areas of research include radon and indoor air pollution, asbestos and lead exposure, acid aerosols, methyl mercury in fish populations, and the long-range health implications of oil spills. With global change and ozone depletion high on the national agenda, NIEHS has also developed a program to research the impacts on human health of alternative, nonfossil fuels and the consequences of ozone depletion and of chlorofluorocarbons and their potential replacements.

Several university-based Environmental Health Science Centers are supported by NIEHS and work closely with the staff of the Institute and of EPA on current problems (see Table A.1). NIEHS publishes *Environmental Health Perspec-*

Table A1. National Institute of Environmental Health Sciences Research Centers

Center	Location	Estimated FY1992 Budget ($000)
Occupational and Environmental Health	Harvard University, Boston, MA	1,426
Center for Study of the Human Environment	University of Cincinnati, Cincinnati, OH	1,070
Center for Environmental Management	Oregon State University, Corvallis, OR	1,274
Research in the Environmental Health Sciences	New York University Medical Center, New York, NY	2,254
Center for Environmental Toxicology	Vanderbilt University, Nashville, TN	1,329
Environmental Agents: Relation to Human Health Effects	Mt. Sinai School of Medicine, New York, NY	1,467
Trace Contaminants as Environmental Health Hazards to Man	University of Rochester, Rochester, NY	1,404
Environmental Health Sciences Center	University of California, Berkeley, CA	1,058
Environmental Health Sciences Center	MIT, Cambridge, MA	1,117
Environmental Health Sciences Center	John Hopkins University, Baltimore, MD	1,378
Environmental Health Sciences Center	University Medical and Dental School, Piscataway, NJ	1,101
Environmental Health Sciences Center	University of Iowa, Iowa City, IA	651
Duke University Marine Biomedical Center	Duke University, Durham, NC	316
NIEHS Freshwater Biomedical Center Grant	University of Wisconsin, Milwaukee, WI	257
Marine Freshwater Biomedical Center Grant	University of Connecticut, Storrs, CT	300
A Marine and Freshwater Biomedical Science Specialized Center of Research at the Mount Desert Biological Lab	Mt. Desert Island Biological Lab, Mt. Desert, ME	277
NIEHS Marine Freshwater Biomedical Sciences	Oregon State University, Corvallis, OR	255
TOTAL		16,934

tives, a widely distributed peer-reviewed journal that deals with both longstanding and newly discovered problems. Finally, NIEHS supports pre- and postdoctoral training in environmental health sciences.

The National Center for Toxicology Research (NCTR) in the Food and Drug Administration, the Agency for Toxic Substances and Disease Registry (ATSDR), the Center for Environmental Health and Injury Control (CEHIC) and the National Institute for Occupational Safety and Health (NIOSH), both within the Centers for Disease Control, all have research programs in environmental health. Located in Jefferson, Arkansas, the National Center for Toxicology Research (NCTR) serves as the basic research arm for the Food and Drug Administration. Its primary mission is to study the biological effects of potentially toxic chemical substances found in the environment, emphasizing the determination of the health effects resulting from the long-term, low-level exposure to toxicants and the basic biological processes for chemical toxicants in animal organisms. One of the major goals of NCTR is to test the assumptions of underlying toxicological risk assessments. Another participant in the effort to assess the impact of toxic chemicals on human health is CEHIC. ATSDR is mandated by the Superfund laws to examine the health effects of exposure to hazardous substances. It also publishes toxicological profiles, health assessments, exposure assessments, and community registries.

The National Toxicology Program, established in 1978 and administered by the director of NIEHS, aims to coordinate the various toxicological programs within HHS and serves as the principal toxicological testing program. The program is designed to evaluate the effects of potentially toxic compounds and to develop and validate new and better toxicological test methods. It also disseminates the results to the academic, commercial, and regulatory communities and to the public.

Another aspect of health research is those activities that have an impact on the day-to-day occupational environment of workers in the U.S. The mission of the National Institute of Occupational Safety and Health is to manage "a national program of occupational safety and health research . . . to estimate and disseminate scientific and public health information to ensure safe and healthful working conditions. . . ."[110] The work at NIOSH supports the Occupational Safety and Health Administration. Engineers, epidemiologists, physicians, and toxicologists seek to identify work-related injuries and illness, assess the toxicity of hazardous material found in the workplace, and evaluate the causes of the ten leading work-related diseases and injuries. The ultimate goal of the NIOSH research program is to provide the basis for preventing occupational illness and injury. In 1992, $93 million was spent on research at NIOSH.

DEPARTMENT OF AGRICULTURE

The U.S. Department of Agriculture (USDA) houses environment-related research in two divisions: the U.S. Forest Service and the Agricultural Research Service. The U.S. Forest Service (USFS), as part of its mission to oversee the management and use of the nation's 1.6 billion acres of forest land, provides scientific and technical information through its Forest Research program. The Forest Service appropriation was $115 million in 1992. A network of 9 experiment stations and 183 research units conduct research in timber management, forest products and harvesting, forest protection, resource analysis research, and forest environmental research. The Forest Service research program focuses on "national problem" areas, including tropical forestry, recycling, and the ecological and social values of forest land.

The Agricultural Research Service (ARS) provides the scientific basis for the production of agricultural commodities that demonstrate wise management and use of the environment; its work has undergirded the major advances in the volume of food and fiber for national and international consumption. Studies of soil erosion, pesticides and fertilizer, and irrigation constitute the bulk of the research program. ARS is also a participant in the global change research program, investigating potential effects of climate change on the nation's agriculture. ARS's funding of $162 million in 1992 supported the eight area offices that coordinate 126 field experiment stations around the country.

The Cooperative State Research Service (CSRS) administers the Department of Agriculture's grant programs for agricultural research. More than half of CSRS's grants are distributed by formula to agricultural research programs at agricultural experiment stations, approved schools of forestry under the Cooperative Forestry program, 1890 land grant colleges, and Tuskegee University. Matching funds are required from all but the land grant colleges and Tuskegee University. Funding for formula grants has remained stable in recent years. CSRS nonformula grants for environmental R&D, including competitive grants and Special Research Grants through itemized appropriations, increased considerably between 1990 and 1992. Total CSRS funding for FY 1992 was an estimated $119 million.[111]

In addition to its funding for the Agricultural Research Service ($162 million), the Cooperative Research Service ($119 million), and the Forest Service ($115 million), the Department's Economic Research Service spent an estimated $7 million in FY 1992 on economic research related to natural resource management.[112] All told, the Department of Agriculture devoted an estimated $403 million to environment-related R&D in FY 1992.

Following the recommendations of a report published in 1989 by the National Research Council regarding the need to strengthen the agricultural research system, USDA has proposed a National Research Initiative.[113] This initiative calls for $500 million in new research grants over a period of ten years to focus on basic rather than applied research and on agricultural productivity rather than production; the grants would be made in the areas of natural resources and the environment, nutrition, food quality and health, animal systems, and plant systems.

The NRC has also looked more specifically at the need to study and integrate alternative agricultural practices.[114] Citing EPA's finding that agriculture is the largest nonpoint source of surface water pollution, the NRC sought to examine "alternative" agricultural processes—that is, those practices that have the goals of reducing input costs, preserving the resource base, and protecting human health. Alternative agriculture includes practices such as crop rotation, integrated pest management, soil- and water-conserving tillage, and genetic improvement of crops. The NRC found, among other things, that only a small number of U.S. farmers currently use alternative farming systems, in large part because federal policies work against environmentally benign practices.

Plant biology research is the subject of another National Research Council report that was requested by NSF, USDA, and DoE. The study examines the mechanisms of research funding, the balance of plant biology research between basic and applied research, and the commitment to building and maintaining a strong infrastructure and personnel base.[115] The report recommends establishing a National Institute of Plant Biology within USDA, promoting better cooperation among agencies engaged in plant biology research, and forming an independent advisory group of nongovernment scientists to help give direction and focus to USDA's research program.

Like EPA, USDA has been criticized for concentrating its efforts on short-term, applied research to the detriment of a basic research program. The National Research Initiative and the efforts to study alternative agriculture and plant biology aim to overcome this criticism and fill voids in the current USDA research program.

DEPARTMENT OF DEFENSE

The Department of Defense (DoD) houses a considerable environmental research program involving all three branches of the military. This program is divided into two major categories: the natural environment and environmental quality. Researchers evaluate the natural environment in order to gather information necessary for defense operations. Research related to environmental quality addresses the countless training, testing, storage, and disposal sites used by the military in its routine activities. R&D efforts are required to maintain and improve the environmental quality of those sites.[116] The Deputy Assistant Secretary of Defense (Environment) provides guidance and broad research coordination between the services, although individual projects are fairly autonomous. Environmental R&D spending at DoD totaled nearly $600 million in 1992.

The largest environmental research program at DoD is within the Office of Naval Research (ONR) in the Department of the Navy. ONR's mission is basic research, which it supports through grants to universities and industry at a funding level of approximately $500 million per year. Oceanography is the primary focus of the ONR research program, including ocean pollution from ships, marine meteorology, and research on tides. ONR also conducts arctic research with an emphasis on ice flows and ocean conditions beneath arctic ice.

Senator Sam Nunn and others have led an effort to redirect a significant amount of DoD resources toward a Strategic Environmental Research and Development Program (SERDP). This initiative proposes that the capabilities of the defense establishment be used now for existing environmental cleanup activities and in the longer term for understanding environmental problems such as global climate change, deforestation, and population growth. The new focus on environmental R&D within the Defense Department would be accomplished by utilizing information gathered by intelligence sources, by sharing previously inaccessible data gathered from military aircraft, ships, and submarines with environmental researchers, and by providing access to DoD supercomputers for modeling and data analysis.

The U.S. Army Corps of Engineers is an important contributor to environment-related research at DoD. The Corps is specifically responsible for two of the twenty-eight technical areas slated for research under SERDP, civil engineering and environmental quality. The Corps also houses an active wetlands study program.

SMITHSONIAN INSTITUTION

The Smithsonian Institution is home to a wide range of research and educational organizations, including fourteen museums and research stations worldwide. Although overall funding for environmental research is modest in comparison to some other agencies—$33 million in 1992—the diverse components of the Smithsonian study a great many environmental topics. Seven research bureaus conduct most of the environmental research programs: the National Air and Space Museum, the National Museum of American History, the National Museum of Natural History, the National Zoological Park, the Smithsonian Astrophysical Observatory, the Smithsonian Environmental Research Center, and the Smithsonian Tropical Research Institute.[117] For example, the Smithsonian Environmental Research Center, on the Chesapeake Bay in Maryland, focuses on landscape ecology—the environmental interaction between ecosystems and habitats, with a special emphasis on wetlands—and the Smithsonian Tropical Research Institute, headquartered in Panama, studies the ecology, behavior, and evolution of tropical organisms and the impact of past and present human activity on tropical ecosystems. The National Museum of Natural History has the largest budget for environmental R&D, about $22 million in 1992. Its research includes extensive programs on biodiversity, systematics, paleoecology, and the interactions between humans and nature.

OTHER AGENCIES

A number of other federal agencies operate small programs that are related to environmental R&D, including the Agency for International Development, the Tennessee Valley Authority, and the Department of Transportation.

The Agency for International Development (AID) supports environment-related research in agricultural and natural resource development. A large portion of this program is devoted to research on the social and economic aspects of environmental issues. AID's environmental R&D program is largely applied and largely extramural, totaling $45 million in 1992.

The Tennessee Valley Authority (TVA) conducts environment-related R&D primarily at its National Fertilizer and Environmental Research Center, founded in 1991. This center focuses on R&D related to water quality and soil nutrients. TVA also conducts research on regional and power development issues. Total environmental R&D spending at TVA in 1992 was $31 million.

Environmental R&D at the Department of Transportation (DoT) is performed by the Coast Guard, the Federal Highway Administration, and the Federal Aviation Administration. The Coast Guard's R&D program is focused on oil spills and pollution, while the Federal Highway Administration's R&D addresses air pollution from highway vehicles and the environmental impacts of other aspects of highway operations, such as noise and runoff. The Federal Aviation Administration's environmental R&D efforts seek to reduce noise and fuel emissions from aircraft. Total environmental R&D funding at DoT was about $17 million in 1992.

APPENDIX B
BIOGRAPHIES OF TASK FORCE MEMBERS

Douglas M. Costle is a former administrator of the U.S. Environmental Protection Agency and former dean of Vermont Law School. Mr. Costle has also been a trial attorney in the Civil Rights Division of the U.S. Department of Justice and has served as an attorney for the U.S. Department of Commerce, Economic Development Administration. He worked as an associate with two San Francisco law firms before becoming senior staff associate to the President's Advisory Council on Executive Organization, in Washington, DC, where he played a key role in establishing the U.S. Environmental Protection Agency. Mr. Costle has served as commissioner of the Connecticut Department of Environmental Protection, as assistant director of the U.S. Congressional Budget Office, and as a fellow of the Smithsonian Institution's Woodrow Wilson International Center for Scholars. He was EPA Administrator from 1977 to 1981. Mr. Costle has also been a visiting scholar at the Harvard School of Public Health and an adjunct lecturer in the John F. Kennedy School of Government. He is a graduate of Harvard University and the University of Chicago Law School.

Robert W. Fri is president of Resources for the Future, an independent nonprofit organization that conducts research and policy analysis on issues affecting natural resources and environmental quality. He received a BA with Honors in Physics from Rice University and an MBA from Harvard. From 1971 to 1975 he served as first deputy administrator and then as acting administrator of the Environmental Protection Agency. From 1975 to 1977 he served as first deputy administrator and then as acting administrator of the Energy Research and Development Administration. Before joining Resources for the Future he was a member of the management consulting firm McKinsey and Company and was president of the Energy Transition Corporation, which engaged in new energy product development. He is a trustee of the Environment and Energy Study Institute, Science Service, Inc., and the Atlantic Council of the U.S. and a member of the Advisory Council of the Electric Power Research Institute, Phi Beta Kappa, and Sigma Xi.

Edward A. Frieman is director of the Scripps Institution of Oceanography, and Vice Chancellor, Marine Sciences of the University of California, San Diego. Before joining Scripps, he was executive vice president of Science Applications International. He formerly was director of Energy Research for the U.S. Department of Energy. He was a professor of astrophysical sciences and deputy director of the Plasma Physics Laboratory at Princeton University from 1952 to 1979. He is a member of the National Academy of Sciences, the American Association for the Advancement of Science, the American Physical Society, the American Philosophical Society, and Sigma Xi.

Stephen J. Gage is president of the Cleveland Advanced Manufacturing Program in Cleveland, Ohio. From 1977 to 1980 he was assistant administrator for research and development of the U.S. Environmental Protection Agency. He received his BS in Mechanical Engineering from the University of Nebraska, and an MS and PhD in Nuclear Engineering from Purdue University. From 1965 to 1971 he was director of the Nuclear Reactor Laboratory at the University of Texas at Austin. His private-sector experience includes positions with Baxter Travenol, where he worked on computer-aided design and manufacturing, and International Harvester, where he was in charge of advanced engineering research. Prior to his current position, Dr. Gage was president of the Indiana Corporation for Science and Technology, which promotes economic development and growth in the areas of science and technology for the State of Indiana. He was a staff member of the Council on Environmental Quality and Director of the Interagency Energy–Environment R&D Program at the U.S. Environmental Protection Agency, where he later served as deputy assistant administrator for Energy, Minerals, and Industry R&D.

Bruce W. Karrh is vice president for safety, health, and environmental affairs at the Du Pont Company. He has been with Du Pont since 1970. He received his MD from the Medical College of Alabama at Birmingham. He is vice chairman of the company's Environmental Leadership Committee and chairman of the Environmental Resources Committee. He is a fellow of the American College of Occupational Medicine and the American College of Preventive Medicine. Dr. Karrh is a member of the board of directors of the American Industrial Health Council, the Institute for Cooperative Environmental management, the Global Tomorrow Coalition, and the Chemical Industry Institute of Toxicology.

Gordon J. F. MacDonald is a professor at the University of California, San Diego Graduate School of International Relations and Pacific Studies, and the director for environmental policy studies at the University of California's Institute on Global Conflict and Cooperation. He received his AB, AM, and PhD from Harvard University. Dr. MacDonald served Presidents Eisenhower and Kennedy as staff associate for the new National Aeronautics and Space Administration and was appointed in 1965 to the President's Science Advisory Committee, where his principle work focused on oceanography, naval warfare, and strategic policies. He was appointed to the first Council on Environmental Quality by President Nixon. He has also served on the Department of State's Advisory Committee on Science and Foreign Affairs and the Defense Science Board, among other bodies. He is a member of the Department of State's Advisory Committee on Oceans and International Environmental and Scientific Affairs.

Gilbert S. Omenn is professor of medicine (medical genetics) and of environmental health and dean of the School of Public Health and Community Medicine at the University of Washington, Seattle. He is principal investigator of the Carotene and Retinol Efficacy Trial (CARET) to prevent lung cancer and director of the Center for Health Promotion in Older Adults. Dr. Omenn served as deputy to Frank Press, President Carter's Science and Technology Advisor and director of the White House Office of Science and Technology Policy, and then as an associate director of the Office of Management and Budget. He was a visiting senior fellow at the Woodrow Wilson School of Public and International Affairs, Princeton University; later, he was the first Science and Public Policy Fellow at The Brookings Institution, Washington, DC. He was elected to membership in the Institute of Medicine and served on its Council. He has chaired the Board of Environmental Studies and Toxicology of the National Research Council, and the Electric Power Research Institute's EMF Health Effects Technical Advisory Board. He serves on the board of directors of Rohm & Haas Company, Amgen, Immune Response Corporation, and the RAND Critical Technologies Institute. He was a White House Fellow at the Atomic Energy Commission. He received his AB from Princeton, his MD from Harvard, and his PhD in Genetics from the University of Washington.

David P. Rall served as director of the National Institute of Environmental Health Sciences from 1971 to 1991. He received his MD and PhD from Northwestern University in 1951. He interned on the Second (Cornell) Medical Division in 1952–1953, and then joined the National Cancer Institute (NCI) as an officer in the United States Public Health Service (Assistant Surgeon General). His early research dealt with anticancer drugs, including treatment of meningeal leukemia in children. The success of this treatment was critical to the cure of some forms of acute leukemia in children. At NCI he was responsible for the preclinical toxicology of the anti-cancer drugs being developed, and he became interested in predictive toxicology and population toxicology. Dr. Rall became director of the National Institute of Environmental Health Sciences in 1971. He also served as the director of the National Toxicology Program.

H. Guyford Stever, a member of the Carnegie Commission on Science, Technology, and Government, was director of the National Science Foundation from 1972 to 1976; during this time he also served as Science Advisor to Presidents Nixon and Ford. Dr. Stever was director of the White House Office of Science and Technology Policy from 1976 to 1977. Before joining NSF, he was a professor at MIT from 1945 to 1965 and president of Carnegie Mellon University from 1965 to 1972. Dr. Stever was Chief Scientist of the U.S. Air Force in 1955–1956. During World War II, in 1941 and 1942, he taught and did research in radar at the MIT Radiation Laboratory, and from 1943 to 1945 was scientific liaison officer on radar and guided missiles in the London Mission of the Office of Scientific Research and Development, including seven technical intelligence missions to the continent of Europe. In the past decade he is or has been a director of TRW Inc., Schering-Plough Corporation, and Goodyear Tire and Rubber Company; a trustee of Woods Hole Oceanographic Institute, and of Science Service, president and trustee of Universities Research Association, and foreign secretary of the National Academy of Engineering. He received his PhD in Physics from the California Institute of Technology. In 1991 he received the National Medal of Science, the nation's highest honor to a scientist, awarded by the President.

Gilbert F. White is a professor emeritus at the Institute of Behavioral Sciences, University of Colorado, Boulder. He received his SB, SM, and PhD from the University of Chicago. He was a geographer with the Mississippi Valley Committee, the Natural Resources Committee, and the National Resources Planning Board. He worked in the Bureau of Budget, Executive Office of the President, from 1940 to 1942 and was President of Haverford College from 1946 to 1955. Dr. White has also been a professor of Geography, University of Chicago; vice chair, President's Water Resources Policy Commission, 1950; and a member of the UNESCO Advisory Committee on Arid Zone Research (1953–1956) and the UNESCO Advisory Committee on Natural Resources Research (1967–1971). He is currently a member of the Advisory Group on Greenhouse Gases, the World Meteorological Organization, the United Nations Environment Program (UNEP), and the Advisory Committee on Environment of the International Council of Scientific Unions. He received the Tyler Prize for Environmental Achievement in 1992.

Mark Schaefer is senior staff associate and director of the Washington office of the Carnegie Commission on Science, Technology, and Government. He received his PhD in the neurosciences from Stanford University in 1987. After completing his undergraduate degree at the University of Washington in 1977, he worked for five years in the Office of Research and Development of the U.S. Environmental Protection Agency. Dr. Schaefer was on the staff of the Congressional Office of Technology Assessment from 1987 to 1989, first as a Congressional Science Fellow and later as project director of OTA's study of the effects of toxic chemicals on the nervous system. From late 1989 to early 1990 he was a Guest Scholar at the Brookings Institution. Since 1988, he has taught an environmental policy tutorial for Stanford University's Washington program.

NOTES AND REFERENCES

1. Carnegie Commission on Science, Technology, and Government, *E³: Organizing for Environment, Energy, and the Economy in the Executive Branch of the U.S. Government*, September 1991, p. 2.

2. Carnegie Commission on Science, Technology, and Government, *Enabling the Future: Linking Science and Technology to Societal Goals*, September 1992.

3. The National Commission on the Environment, chaired by Russell Train, is sponsored by the World Wildlife Fund headquartered in Washington, DC. Its report, *Choosing a Sustainable Future* (Island Press, Washington, DC, in press), is expected to be published in January 1993.

4. If a U.S. Environmental Monitoring Agency is established, as recommended later in this report, some of the activities of a proposed National Environmental Monitoring Systems Laboratory (NEMSL) should be integrated with those of, or transferred to, the new agency.

5. This Task Force did not examine the issue of the organization of a Department of the Environment. For an in-depth discussion of the potential structure of such a department, we refer the reader to the report by the National Commission on the Environment, cited in note 3, above.

6. National Library of Medicine, Planning Panel on Toxicology and Environmental Health, *Report to the Board of Regents of the National Library of Medicine*, Bethesda, Maryland, September 1992.

7. Cheryl Simon Silver with Ruth S. DeFries, *One Earth, One Future: Our Changing Global Environment*, National Academy Press, Washington, DC, 1990, p. 15.

8. *The State of the Environment*, Organization for Economic Cooperation and Development, Paris, 1991, pp. 283–284.

9. Paul C. Stern, Oran R. Young, and Daniel Druckman, editors, *Global Environment Change: Understanding the Human Dimension*, National Academy Press, Washington, DC, 1992, p. 17.

10. *Ibid.*

11. L. Arizpe, R. Constanza, and W. Lutz, "Primary Factors Affecting Population and Natural Resource Use," Report from the International Conference on an Agenda of Science for Environment and Development, Vienna, Austria, November 24–29, 1991, p. 2.

12. *Ibid.*

13. In Cheryl Simon Silver with Ruth S. DeFries, *op. cit.*, note 7 above.

14. George Brown, "Global Change and the New Definition of Progress," a speech before the Annual Meeting of the Geological Society of America, October 21, 1991, pp. 5–6.

15. Michael Kowalok, "The Origin and Progress of Scientific Findings on Critical Environmental Issues," background paper prepared for the Carnegie Commission on Science, Technology, and Government, 1992.

16. Mark Schaefer, "The Federal Research Puzzle: Making the Pieces Fit," *Environment* 33(9): 16–20; 38–42, 1991. Steven J. Kafka, "Federal Environment Research and Development Programs: Organizational Policy Issues for the 1990s and Beyond," background paper prepared for the Carnegie Commission on Science, Technology, and Government, 1991.

17. For a detailed discussion, see Steven J. Kafka, *op. cit.*, note 16 above.

18. D. Allan Bromley, "A Science and Technology Policy for the 1990's," address to the AAAS Colloquium on Science and Technology Policy, Washington, DC, April 16, 1992.

19. When the Environmental Protection Agency was established in 1970, its original mandate was to take a long-term view of the overall condition of the environment and its capacity to support a health life for all species—including human beings. However, in the years that followed, Congress gave EPA a plethora of very specific regulatory responsibilities. These added duties have weakened EPA's ability to do comprehensive long-range planning and to look at the "big picture." See, for example, Chapter 2 of *Future Risk: Research Strategies for the 1990s*, U.S. EPA, Science Advisory Board, September 1988, SAB-EC-88-040.

20. *Environmental Research and Assessment: Proposals for Better Organization and Decision Making*, Carnegie Commission on Science, Technology, and Government, July 1992.

21. Carnegie Commission on Science, Technology, and Government, *op. cit.*, note 1 above, p. 14.

22. Office of Management and Budget, *Budget of the U.S. Government FY 1993*, U.S. Government Printing Office, Washington, DC, p. 131.

23. World Resources Institute, *Backs to the Future: U.S. Government Policy toward Environmentally Critical Technology*, Washington, DC, June 1992, p. 19.

24. Harvey Brooks, "Innovation and Competitiveness," a symposium lecture in memory of J. Herbert Hollomon, April 9, 1991.

25. Carnegie Commission on Science, Technology, and Government, *Technology and Economic Performance: Organizing the Executive Branch for a Stronger National Technology Base*, New York, September 1991.

26. Congressional Research Service, *Federal R&D in Environmental Technologies*, July 17, 1992, p. 6.

27. Jonathon Parker, "Environmental Assessment: Two Conferences on Environmental Indicators and Indices," *Environment* 33(5):41–43, 1991.

28. Office of Management and Budget, *Budget of the United States Government, Fiscal Year 1993*, U.S. Government Printing Office, Washington, DC, 1992, p. 397.

29. For example, despite a growth in EPA program responsibilities during the 1980s, the EPA operating budget fell from $1.7 billion in 1979 to $1.0 billion in 1983, and only increased to $1.7 billion again in 1991 (in constant 1982 dollars). See GAO/RCED-91-97.

30. Edward S. Rubin, Lester B. Lave, and M. Granger Morgan, "Keeping Climate Research Relevant," *Issues in Science and Technology* 8(2):47–55, 1992.

31. Jonathon Parker, *op. cit.*, note 27 above, p. 42.

32. U.S. Environmental Protection Agency, *Unfinished Business*, Washington, DC, 1987, p. 97.

33. Charles W. Powers, "The Role of NGOs in Improving the Employment of Science and Technology in Environmental Management," background paper for the Carnegie Commission on Science, Technology, and Government, Task Force on Nongovernmental Organizations, 1991.

34. Committee for the NIE, "National Institutes for the Environment: A Proposal," Washington, DC, 1992.

35. The Environmental Quality Improvement Act of 1970 (Public Law 91-224) established the Office of Environmental Quality: "There is established in the Executive Office of the President an office to be known as the Office of Environmental Quality. . . . The Chairman of the Council on Environmental Quality established by Public Law 91-190 shall be the Director of the Office. There shall be in the Office a Deputy Director who shall be appointed by the President, by and with the advice and consent of the Senate."

36. Carnegie Commission on Science, Technology, and Government, *op. cit.*, note 1 above.

37. Mark Schaefer, "Bridging the Environmental Research/Policy Interface: Three Organizational and Procedural Proposals," presented at the Annual Meeting of the American Association for the Advancement of Science, February 10, 1992.

38. Robert W. Fri, "Used and Useful: Science, Technology, and Policy," remarks presented at the Electric Power Research Institute Board of Directors/Advisory Council Summer Seminar, August 10, 1992.

39. Schaefer, *op. cit.*, note 37 above.

40. National Commission on the Environment, *op. cit.*, note 3 above.

41. Carnegie Commission on Science, Technology, and Government, *op. cit.*, note 2 above.

42. Office of Science and Technology Policy, "Our Changing Planet: The FY 1991 U.S. Global Change Research Program," a report by the Committee on Earth Sciences, Federal Coordinating Council for Science, Engineering, and Technology.

43. William D. Ruckelshaus, "Risk, Science, and Democracy," *Issues in Science and Technology* 1(3):19–38, 1985.

44. U.S. Environmental Protection Agency, "Safeguarding the Future: Credible Science, Credible Decisions," EPA/600/9-91/050, March 1992.

45. Letter to the Honorable Edward P. Boland, Chairman, House Appropriations Subcommittee on VA, HUD, and Independent Agencies, April 5, 1984.

46. Ralph de Gennaro, Friends of the Earth, testimony before the House Committee on Science, Space, and Technology, March 19, 1992.

47. U.S. House of Representatives, Committee on Science, Space, and Technology, "The Role of Science at EPA and Fiscal Year 1993 Budget Authorization for EPA's Office of Research and Development," Hearing, March 19, 1992, No. 129, U.S. Government Printing Office, Washington, DC.

48. After the Task Force drafted its proposal for combining the USGS and NOAA, it was brought to a Task Force member's attention that a similar proposal had been developed by a USGS employee in 1987. The USGS Chief Geologist, Robert M. Hamilton, wrote an internal memorandum (dated January 16, 1987) in which he stated: "Program coordination and integration with NOAA are potentially so important that they deserve special consideration. In reality, the USGS has more programmatic interests in common with NOAA than with other DOI bureaus. I believe that integration of USGS and NOAA information and data services should be seriously evaluated. Moreover, I think consideration should be given to combining USGS and NOAA to form a new organization." Dr. Hamilton went on to suggest the new organization be called the National Earth Science and Technology Administration (NESTA).

Indeed, Dr. Hamilton sought and received confirmation from Walter J. Hickel, Sr., former Secretary of the Interior (in a letter dated June 18, 1986), that during the Nixon Administration serious consideration had been given to placing NOAA in the Department of the Interior.

49. For an independent evaluation of the EMAP Program, see "Review of EPA's Environmental Monitoring and Assessment Program (EMAP): Interim Report," National Research Council, Washington, DC, June 1992.

50. Information on *Arctic Data Interactive: A Prototype CD-ROM Science Journal* may be obtained from the Information Systems Division, U.S. Geological Survey, 801 National Center, Reston, VA, 22092.

51. *U.S. Geological Survey Yearbook, Fiscal Year 1991*, p. 24.

52. Committee on Merchant Marine and Fisheries, Subcommittee on Oceanography and Great Lakes, H.R. Rept. 101-92 (Status of NOAA in the Department of Commerce) 101st Cong., 2nd Sess. at 31–33 (May 8, 1990).

53. Department of Commerce, "NOAA Ship to Survey Persian Gulf Oil Spills," Press Release NIL 92-2 (January 8, 1992).

54. Department of Commerce, "More Damaging Gases Reaching Ozone Than Originally Thought," Press Release NIL 91-72 (July 30, 1991).

55. Robert G. Fleagle, "The Case for a New NOAA Charter," *Bulletin of the American Meteorological Society* 68:1417, 1422, 1987. In fact, in 1983 the Office of Management and Budget required that NOAA no longer identify its research as "basic."

56. Testimony of Martin H. Belsky in Committee on Merchant Marine and Fisheries, Subcommittee on Oceanography and Great Lakes, H.R. Rept. 101-92 (Status of NOAA in the Department of Commerce) 101st Cong., 2nd Sess. at 20-23 (May 8, 1990).

57. Robert G. Fleagle, "The U.S. Government Response to Global Change: Analysis and Appraisal," *Global Change* 20:57–81, 1992.

58. According to the 1992 Appropriations Committee hearings, much of NOAA's environmental data "is at serious risk due to deteriorating storage media." NOAA estimates that approximately half of its on-hand data is presently unusable. Also, the National Weather Service has requested approximately $55 million for modernization, including an increase for Next Generation Radar (NEXRAD), Automated Surface Observing System (ASOS), and purchase of a class IV supercomputer. *See* Committee on Appropriations, Subcommittee on the Department of Commerce, Justice, and State, the Judiciary, and Related Agencies, Hearings before a Subcommittee of the Committee on Appropriations (Part I), 102nd Cong., 1st sess. (1991).

59. Fleagle, *op. cit.*, note 55 above.

60. National Commission on the Environment, *op. cit.*, note 3 above.

61. Dr. Peter Raven, Director of the Missouri Botanical Garden, and others have described the need for national biological inventories.

62. Congressional Research Service, "Federal R&D in Environmental Technologies," coordinated by John D. Moteff, July 17, 1992.

63. Marc H. Ross and Robert H. Socolow, "Fulfilling the Promise of Environmental Technology," *Issues in Science and Technology* 7(3):61–66, 1991.

64. Robert W. Fri, "Organizing Federal Programs to Support the Development of Environmental Technologies," testimony before the U.S. Senate Committee on Governmental Affairs, July 21, 1992.

65. Harvey Brooks, "Innovation and Competitiveness," a symposium lecture in memory of J. Herbert Holloman, April 9, 1991.

66. The Office of National Environmental Technologies Act of 1992 (H.R. 5959) was introduced by Congressman Joseph P. Kennedy on September 16, 1992.

67. U.S. General Accounting Office, Earth Observing System: NASA's EOSDIS Development Approach Is Risky, GAO/IMTEC-92-24, Washington, DC, February 1992.

68. Kenneth Olden, National Institute of Environmental Health Sciences, "Environmental Research and Education: Needs and Opportunities," prepared for the University Colloquium on Environmental Research and Education, Raleigh, North Carolina, September 24–26, 1992.

69. Public Health Service, Department of Health and Human Services, Evaluating the Environmental Health Work Force, publication HRP 0907160, January 1988.

70. National Research Council, Board on Environmental Studies and Toxicology, *Science in the National Parks*, National Academy Press, Washington, DC, 1992.

71. *Ibid.*

72. *Ibid.*

73. National Research Council, Board on Environmental Studies and Toxicology, *Hazardous Materials on the Public Lands*, National Academy Press, Washington, DC, 1992.

74. *Ibid.*

75. National Research Council, *Investing in Research: A Proposal to Strengthen the Agricultural, Food, and Environmental System*, National Academy Press, Washington, DC, 1989.

76. Office of Technology Assessment, *Agricultural Research and Technology Transfer Policies for the 1990s*, March 1990, pp. 3, 7.

77. Carnegie Commission on Science, Technology, and Government, *op. cit.*, note 1 above.

78. Draft Final Report of the Secretary of Energy Advisory Board Task Force on the Department of Energy National Laboratories, January 29, 1992.

79. Executive Office of the President, *U.S. Actions for a Better Environment: A Sustained Commitment*, Washington, DC, 1992.

80. International Conference on an Agenda of Science for Environment and Development into the 21st Century (ASCEND 21), Vienna, Austria, November 25–29, 1991, organized by the International Council of Scientific Unions (ICSU) in cooperation with the Third World Academy of Sciences (TWAS).

81. S. 2866, introduced in the 102nd Congress, establishes a program to assist in the deployment of energy and environmental practices and technologies; the program would be called the "ADEPT" program.

82. Carnegie Commission on Science, Technology, and Government, *International Environmental Research and Assessment: Proposals for Better Organization and Decision Making*, July 1991, p. 22.

83. Alexander Keynan, "The United States as a Partner in Scientific and Technological Cooperation: Some Perspectives from Across the Atlantic," Consultant report to the Carnegie Commission on Science, Technology, and Government, June 1991.

84. U.S. Environmental Protection Agency, *Unfinished Business*, Washington, DC, 1987.

85. U.S. Environmental Protection Agency, *Reducing Risk: Setting Priorities and Strategies for Environmental Protection*, Washington, DC, September 1990.

86. Ecological Society of America, "Sustainable Biosphere Initiative: An Unecological Research Agenda," reprinted from *Ecology* 72(2), April 1991.

87. Carnegie Commission on Science, Technology, and Government, *The Limits of Government in Science and Technology: Roles and Challenges for Nongovernmental Organizations*, in press.

88. Charles W. Powers, *op. cit.*, note 33, above.

89. *Ibid.*

90. Kathleen M. Gramp, Albert H. Teich, and Stephen D. Nelson, "Federal Funding of Environmental R&D," a report to the National Academy of Sciences and the Carnegie Commission on Science, Technology, and Government by the American Association for the Advancement of Science.

91. A number of these programs were discussed at the University Colloquium on Environmental Research and Education held in Raleigh, North Carolina, on September 24–26, 1992. Information on the proceedings of the Colloquium may be obtained from Sigma Xi, the Scientific Research Society, 99 Alexander Drive, PO Box 13975, Research Triangle Park, NC 27709.

92. Lester R. Brown, "Launching the Environmental Revolution," in *State of the World 1992*, Worldwatch Institute, W. W. Norton, New York, 1992, p. 175.

93. Jim MacNeill, Director of the Environment and Sustainable Development Program at the Institute for Research on Public Policy in Ottawa, Canada, quoted in Cheryl Simon Silver with Ruth S. DeFries, *op. cit.*, note 7 above, p. 60.

94. *Regulatory Program of the U.S. Government, 1 April 1990 – 31 March 1991*, p. vii.

95. Steven J. Kafka, *op. cit.*, note 16 above, Figure 3, p. 10.

96. *An Evaluation of EPA's Exploratory Grants Program*, a report prepared for OER by American Management Systems, Inc., April 1988.

97. National Academy of Public Administration, *EPA's Office of Research and Development: Leadership and Staff for a New Agenda*, July 1990.

98. *An Evaluation of EPA's Exploratory Research Grants Program, op. cit.*, note 96 above.

99. U.S. Environmental Protection Agency, *Safeguarding the Future: Credible Science, Credible Decisions*, March 1992.

100. National Research Council, *Environmental Monitoring and Assessment Program: Interim Report*, National Academy Press, Washington, DC, June 1992.

101. National Science Foundation FY 1992 Budget Justification.

102. This figure does not include $265 million to support the National Environment Satellite, Data, and Information Service.

103. Robert E. Chapman, U.S. Department of Commerce, "Benefit–Cost Analysis for the Modernization and Associated Restructuring of the National Weather Service," NISTIR 4867, July 1992.

104. Gramp *et al.*, *op. cit.*, note 90 above.

105. Department of the Interior FY 1992 Budget Justification.

106. National Research Council, Committee to Review the Outer Continental Shelf Environmental Studies Program, *The Adequacy of Environmental Information for Outer Continental Shelf Oil and Gas Decisions: Florida and California*, National Academy Press, 1989; Physical Oceanography Panel, *Assessment of the U.S. Outer Continental Shelf Environmental Studies Program*, National Academy Press, Washington, DC, 1990; Ecology Panel, *Assessment of the U.S. Outer Continental Shelf Environmental Studies Program*, National Academy Press, Washington, DC, 1992.

107. 43 USC, March 3, 1879.

108. U.S. General Accounting Office, *op. cit.*, note 67 above.

109. NIEHS FY 1992 Budget Justification, p. 121.

110. NIOSH FY 1992 Budget Justification, p. 487.

111. Gramp *et al.*, *op. cit.*, note 90 above.

112. *Ibid.*

113. National Research Council, Board on Agriculture, *Investing in Research: A Proposal to Strengthen the Agricultural, Food, and Environmental System*, National Academy Press, Washington, DC, 1989.

114. National Research Council, *Alternative Agriculture*, National Academy Press, Washington, DC, 1989.

115. National Research Council, *Plant Biology Research and Training for the 21st Century*, National Academy Press, Washington, DC, 1992.

116. Keith Schneider, "Military Has New Strategic Goal in Cleanup of Vast Toxic Waste," *New York Times*, 5 August 1991.

117. Smithsonian Institution Office of Environmental Awareness, "Environmental Conservation Activities at the Smithsonian Institution, 1992–1993."

MEMBERS OF THE CARNEGIE COMMISSION ON SCIENCE, TECHNOLOGY, AND GOVERNMENT

William T. Golden (Co-Chair)
Chairman of the Board
American Museum of Natural History

Joshua Lederberg (Co-Chair)
University Professor
Rockefeller University

David Z. Robinson (Executive Director)
Carnegie Commission on Science,
  Technology, and Government

Richard C. Atkinson
Chancellor
University of California, San Diego

Norman R. Augustine
Chair & Chief Executive Officer
Martin Marietta Corporation

John Brademas
President Emeritus
New York University

Lewis M. Branscomb
Albert Pratt Public Service Professor
Science, Technology, and Public Policy
  Program
John F. Kennedy School of Government
Harvard University

Jimmy Carter
Former President of the United States

William T. Coleman, Jr.
Attorney
O'Melveny & Myers

Sidney D. Drell
Professor and Deputy Director
Stanford Linear Accelerator Center

Daniel J. Evans
Chairman
Daniel J. Evans Associates

General Andrew J. Goodpaster (Ret.)
Chairman
Atlantic Council of The United States

Shirley M. Hufstedler
Attorney
Hufstedler, Kaus & Ettinger

Admiral B. R. Inman (Ret.)

Helene L. Kaplan
Attorney
Skadden, Arps, Slate, Meagher & Flom

Donald Kennedy
Bing Professor of Environmental Science
Institute for International Studies and
President Emeritus
Stanford University

Charles McC. Mathias, Jr.
Attorney
Jones, Day, Reavis & Pogue

William J. Perry
Chairman & Chief Executive Officer
Technology Strategies & Alliances, Inc.

Robert M. Solow
Institute Professor
Department of Economics
Massachusetts Institute of Technology

H. Guyford Stever
Former Director
National Science Foundation

Sheila E. Widnall
Associate Provost and Abby Mauze
  Rockefeller Professor of Aeronautics
  and Astronautics
Massachusetts Institute of Technology

Jerome B. Wiesner
President Emeritus
Massachusetts Institute of Technology

MEMBERS OF THE TASK FORCE ON THE ORGANIZATION OF FEDERAL ENVIRONMENTAL R&D PROGRAMS